the BEST Mentoring Experience

A Framework for Professional Development

Sharon A. Kortman

Connie J. Honaker

 KENDALL/HUNT PUBLISHING COMPANY
4050 Westmark Drive   Dubuque, Iowa 52002

Copyright © 2002 by Kendall/Hunt Publishing Company

ISBN 0-7872-8171-9

All rights reserved. No part of this publication may be reproduced, stored in a retrieval system, or transmitted, in any form or by any means, electronic, mechanical, photocopying, recording, or otherwise, without the prior written permission of the copyright owner.

Permission is hereby granted to participants to reproduce Participant Resources specifically designated in the text for duplication as applicable in classroom quantities for personal, non-commercial use in the classroom.

Printed in the United States of America
10 9 8 7 6 5 4   07 06

About the Authors

Authors and Editors:

Sharon A. Kortman (Ed.D. Curriculum and Instruction) is Lecturer in the College of Education at Arizona State University. She is the Director of Beginning Educator Support Team (BEST), a partnership between university and school districts providing comprehensive support and training in the areas of teacher induction, mentoring and preparation for aligning practice to the teaching standards. She has served in various capacities at all educational levels. She currently teaches Managing the Classroom Culture, Assessment and Supervision of Instruction and trains in all BEST courses for beginning teachers, mentors and professionals evolving in their practice. She is co-author and co-editor of *the BEST Beginning Teacher Experience: Program Facilitator Guide, the BEST Beginning Teacher Experience: A Framework for Professional Development, the BEST Mentoring Experience: Program Facilitator Guide, the BEST Mentoring Experience: A Framework for Professional Development, Trade Secrets for Primary and Elementary Teachers* and *Trade Secrets for Middle and Secondary Teachers.* She is also co-author and co-editor of all BEST Standards in Teaching and Visitation Coach curriculum. Currently her research emphasis is in the areas of attracting and retaining quality teachers and strengthening effective teaching practices. In addition, she consults in the areas of personality and interaction styles, which along with support to the education profession, positively affects student achievement.

Connie J. Honaker (M.A.) is a Faculty Associate for the Beginning Educator Support Team (BEST) program in the College of Education at Arizona State University. She trains in BEST for beginning educators, BEST for mentors, BEST Standards in Teaching and teaches Assessment and Supervision of Instruction. She is co-author and co-editor of *the BEST Beginning Teacher Experience: Program Facilitator Guide, the BEST Beginning Teacher Experience: A Framework for Professional Development, the BEST Mentoring Experience: Program Facilitator Guide, the BEST Mentoring Experience: A Framework for Professional Development, Trade Secrets for Primary and Elementary Teachers* and *Trade Secrets for Middle and Secondary Teachers.* She is also co-author and co-editor of all BEST Standards in Teaching and Visitation Coach curriculum. Connie has taught English and reading at both the elementary and secondary levels. She has served as an administrator in various roles since 1986. Connie is a recipient of the Arizona Distinguished Administrator of the Year Award presented by the Arizona School Administrators Association. There is special pride in her last administrative assignment, where she was founding principal of a large comprehensive high school. All of these roles and her research in teacher induction and mentoring have given her insight into the needs of teachers and administrators and have prepared her for her current position, BEST coordinator and consultant.

Contents

Foreword ix
Preface xi
Acknowledgements xv
Dedication xvi
Introduction xvii
Supplemental Resources xix

CHAPTER 1
Establishing a Mentoring Relationship 1

Planning Calendar 3
    Tip from Mentor Teacher 3
    Check Points 3
    Topics to Discuss with Mentee 3
Professional Development Lesson Plan 4
    Tip 4
    Subject/Class/Period 4
    Objectives 4
    Teaching Standard 4
    Set 4
    Procedures 4
    Self-Assessment/Reflection 5
    Celebration 5
    Extended Activities 5
    Resources 5
Top Ten Needs of Teachers 6
"The Stages of a Teacher's First Year" by Ellen Moir 7
Beginning Teacher Responses to Five Stages of First Year Teaching 9
Behaviors of Effective Mentoring 11
Content Related Reflection 12
Mentor/Mentee Summary of Interaction 13
Interactions Contact Log 14
Choice Activities for Ongoing Professional Development 15
    Classroom Management Tips 15
    Common Questions Asked by New Teachers 15
    Front Office Interview 15
    Time Management Tips 15
Journal 17

CHAPTER 2
Encouraging Teachers through Mentoring 19

Planning Calendar 21
    Tip from Mentor Teacher 21
    Check Points 21
    Topics to Discuss with Mentee 21
Professional Development Lesson Plan 22
    Tip 22
    Subject/Class/Period 22
    Objectives 22
    Teaching Standard 22
    Set 22
    Procedures 22
    Self-Assessment/Reflection 23
    Celebration 23
    Extended Activities 23
    Resources 23
Celebration 24
Using Reflective Questioning to Promote Collaborative Dialogue 25
Reflective Summary Guide 30
Reflective Questioning Role-Play 31
Array Interaction Inventory 33
Array Teacher Scenarios 35
Array Interaction Model Guide 36
Array Proactive Mentoring Plan 37
Array Interaction Inventory (Resource) 38
Content Related Reflection 39
Mentor/Mentee Summary of Interaction 40
Interactions Contact Log 41
Choice Activities for Ongoing Professional Development 42
    Tips for Written Communication to Parents 42
    Tips for Documentation 42
    Teaching Self-Assessment 42
Journal 43

CHAPTER 3
Developing Teaching Skills and Support through Mentoring 45

Planning Calendar 47
- Tip from Mentor Teacher 47
- Check Points 47
- Topics to Discuss with Mentee 47

Professional Development Lesson Plan 48
- Tip 48
- Subject/Class/Period 48
- Objectives 48
- Teaching Standard 48
- Set 48
- Procedures 48
- Self-Assessment/Reflection 49
- Celebration 49
- Extended Activities 49
- Resources 49

Celebration 50

Classroom Data Collection Techniques 51

Sample Feedback: Reinforcement + Refinement 54

Feedback: Reinforcement + Refinement 55

Systemic Support for Teacher Induction and Mentoring 56

Who, What, Where, When and How?: Mentor Brochure 58

Mentoring Commitment Letter 61

Content Related Reflection 62

Mentor/Mentee Summary of Interaction 63

Interactions Contact Log 64

Choice Activities for Ongoing Professional Development 65
- Teacher Seminar 65
- Student Behaviors: Prevention/Intervention 65
- Modeling Professionalism for New Teachers 65

Journal 66

CHAPTER 4
Analyzing and Planning for Professional Growth through Mentoring 67

Planning Calendar 69
- Tip from Mentor Teacher 69
- Check Points 69
- Topics to Discuss with Mentee 69

Professional Development Lesson Plan 70
- Tip 70
- Subject/Class/Period 70
- Objectives 70
- Teaching Standard 70
- Set 70
- Procedures 70
- Self-Assessment/Reflection 71
- Celebration 71
- Extended Activities 71
- Resources 71

Celebration: Mentoring Acrostic 73

Ten Characteristics of Effective Mentoring Relationships 74

How the Mentoring Relationship Facilitates Protégé Growth 75

The Mentoring Cycle 77

Content Related Reflection 79

Mentor/Mentee Summary of Interaction 80

Interactions Contact Log 81

Choice Activities for Ongoing Professional Development 82
- Table Talk: Professional Topic 82
- Systemic View Point 82
- Reflective Questioning Review 82

Journal 84

CHAPTER 5
Strengthening Teacher Practices through Mentoring 85

Planning Calendar 87
    Tip from Mentor Teacher 87
    Check Points 87
    Topics to Discuss with Mentee 87
Professional Development Lesson Plan 88
    Tip 88
    Subject/Class/Period 88
    Objectives 88
    Teaching Standard 88
    Set 88
    Procedures 88
    Self-Assessment/Reflection 89
    Celebration 89
    Extended Activities 89
    Resources 89
Examples of Standards 90
Mentoring by Design 91
    Conference Plan 91
    Role-Play 91
Journal Entry 92
Content Related Reflection 93
Mentor/Mentee Summary of Interaction 94
Interactions Contact Log 95
Choice Activities for Ongoing Professional Development 96
    Classroom Observation 96
    Instructional Design Assistance 96
    Resources for Professional Development 96
Journal 97

CHAPTER 6
Reflecting on the Mentoring Relationship 99

Planning Calendar 101
    Tip from Mentor Teacher 101
    Check Points 101
    Topics to Discuss with Mentee 101
Professional Development Lesson Plan 102
    Tip 102
    Subject/Class/Period 102
    Objectives 102
    Teaching Standards 102
    Set 102
    Procedures 102
    Self-Assessment/Reflection 103
    Celebration 103
    Extended Activities 103
    Resources 103
A Look Back: Mentor Reflection 104
Close Down to Start Up 106
The Future's Here: Professional Growth Plan 107
Content Related Reflection 108
Mentor/Mentee Summary of Interaction 109
Interactions Contact Log 110
Choice Activities for Ongoing Professional Development 111
    Celebration 111
    Assistance with District Procedures 111
    My Own Creation 111
Journal 112

Resources 113

Foreword

From birth we learn through apprenticeship. It is how we become members of our social communities. Parents, siblings, friends and relatives guide our introduction to the mysteries of birthday parties, schooling, sports and dating. Nothing socially complex is learned easily or well without guidance from knowledgeable others. Consequently, those who choose to teach almost always have a long apprenticeship of informal and formal observation in classrooms followed by student teaching. This is their apprenticeship. But then, as novices, when the complexity of the work is most overwhelming, most school districts in America abandon their new teachers. This is shortsighted.

It is now well documented that the craft aspects of teaching are learned in 5–7 years. It is an enormously complex profession requiring intellectual and emotional resources that stretch most people. Evidence is found in the dropout rates of new teachers. In some districts 50% leave the profession during their first five years on the job. Under conditions like these, masters, models, mentors, knowledgeable others, can play an important role in the lives of novice teachers. They can ease the transitions from novice to competent teacher, start the novice on the road to expertise, and provide the emotional and technical scaffolding for the novice to accomplish their initial teaching assignments. Moreover, we have evidence that mentors dramatically reduce the dropout rate of beginning teachers from the profession.

A good mentoring program, then, meets both moral and economic goals. And the one described in this book is just that. Based on ASU's experience over a number of years, we have developed a very good and cost effective mentoring program. Teachers, principals and superintendents who have adopted our mentoring program provide us with remarkably positive feedback that both make us proud and provide the impetus for sharing our program.

BEST (Beginning Educator Support Team) was invented because a complex-to-learn profession such as teaching required it. But in these times of teacher shortages, mentoring programs such as BEST make good economic sense as well. Retaining experienced, competent teachers is much more cost effective than searching for new and less able ones. And the professional development opportunities for the mentor teachers is an additional bonus from a program such as this. It really is time that mentoring programs such as BEST become common in every school district in America.

David C. Berliner
Dean and Regents' Professor
Arizona State University

Preface

Why BEST?

The challenges of attrition, competence and retention of teachers are evident nationwide. The major reasons for high attrition rates of teachers include feelings of isolation, lack of support, challenging assignments due to societal changes and inadequate induction support and mentoring programs (U.S. Department of Education, 1997; Helping New Teachers Succeed, 1994). The U.S. Department of Education predicts a need for approximately 2 million new teachers in the next decade. To respond to this demand, there is a need to address attracting teachers to the profession and address the variables that influence teacher development, and therefore, impact the retention of quality educators.

Research documents a clear link between the importance of teacher induction programs and mentoring programs to the retention and quality of beginning teachers (Odel, 1989; Summers, 1987; Blackburn, 1977; Hegler and Dudrey, 1986). Teacher induction programs "potentially hold a great deal of promise for retaining greater numbers of beginning teachers in the profession and thus reduce the waste of resources and human potential associated with unnecessarily high teacher attrition during the beginning years" (Huling-Austin, 1989).

The revolving door pattern of teachers coming and going negatively effects student achievement (U.S. Department of Education, 1996). According to National Association of Secondary School Principals Newsletter, March 1999, a national survey reported that 70 percent of beginning teachers who were mentored once a week reported a significant improvement in their teaching. The one-on-one support to beginning educators is a critical component to beginning educators' success.

BEST has been developed to assist with these challenges to have the best teachers possible in every classroom for every child. We cannot afford to have less than the BEST.

What Is BEST for Mentor Teachers?

BEST provides support and encouragement for the success and professional development of beginning educators and mentors. BEST is a comprehensive three-year teacher induction and mentoring partnership program. It includes four program components:

- BEST for Beginning Educators
- BEST Classroom Visitation Support
- BEST Standards in Teaching
- BEST for Mentor Teachers

Support is provided for mentor teachers by six seminars throughout the school year, one-on-one beginning teacher/mentor interactions and choice activities that relate to the context of their mentoring practices.

This text correlates with the six mentor teacher seminars. It is also designed as a stand alone text for mentor teachers who are not involved in a district or school organized mentoring program. This component of BEST can be implemented into any mentoring program at a local school, district, through a university partnership or at the state level. This text for mentors provides research based, developmentally appropriate activities for the support of the mentor educator. The chapters lead the mentor through content related to mentor development with working documents, application focus and reflection activities for ongoing professional growth.

By providing opportunities for veterans to increase competence in mentoring practice through knowledge, skill development, application, self-reflection and goal setting, student achievement is positively impacted.

"BEST has provided the opportunity for me to assess and refine my own teaching while I am supporting other teachers. It has been renewing to foster another teacher's growth. Through mentor training a collaborative environment has been built. The staff now reaches out, listens and supports each other."

—BEST Mentor Teacher

Background/History

In the mid '90s, the BEST program was piloted. It was originally designed to provide support to new teachers only and served two urban core districts in the Phoenix area. Over the next few years, the program tripled in size. In the late '90s, additional program components were developed and piloted. They included training for mentor teachers and additional support to beginning teachers through visitation coaches who provided personalized classroom support. In 1999, the fourth component, Standards in Teaching, was implemented, which helped second year teachers and beyond reflect, analyze and document their practice in relationship to teaching standards.

Currently, BEST is partnered with school districts and education agencies. Course credit options are available for master level credit and/or local district credit for all program components. One uniqueness of BEST is that the instructional staff and visitation coaches are embedded within the districts, providing systemic support and a tailored process for induction, mentoring, coaching and staff development. The university partnership provides curriculum, training, consistent support of instructors, research, materials and ongoing program development.

All program components have been field-tested in diverse settings (small to large, urban to rural), researched for ongoing program development, analyzed for effectiveness and aligned with beginning teachers' priority needs. Due to the growing demand for quality teacher induction and mentoring programs, the BEST seminar curriculum for beginning teachers and mentor teachers, with supporting materials, are now available for all districts to use to attract, develop and retain quality teachers for the benefit of student achievement.

BEST for Mentor Teachers

The following topics are presented in *the BEST Mentoring Experience: A Framework for Professional Development*. In addition to content listed below, each chapter includes a calendar, tips for success, content related reflection, journal entry, resources and extended activities.

Establishing a Mentor Relationship

- Getting Acquainted
- Beginning Educator Top Ten Needs
- Phases of First Year Teaching
- Successful Partnerships
- Behaviors of Effective Mentoring

Encouraging Teachers through Mentoring

- Celebration
- Reflective Questioning Reading
- Reflective Questioning Role-Play
- Array Interaction Model
- Reflect and Respond

Developing Teaching Skills and Support through Mentoring

- Classroom Observation Techniques
- Specific Feedback from Reinforcement to Refinement
- Professional Growth through Systemic Support
- Mentoring Commitment Letter

Analyzing and Planning for Professional Growth through Mentoring

- Mentoring Acrostic
- Characteristics of Effective Mentoring
- Elements to Facilitate Mentee Growth
- The Mentoring Cycle

Strengthening Teacher Practices through Mentoring

- Teaching Standards Preview
- Questions to Facilitate Growth
- Mentoring by Design
- Conference Plan
- Journal Entry

Reflecting on the Mentoring Relationship

- Mentor Memory Reflection
- A Look Back
- Closure to the Mentoring Relationship
- Create Mentee's Professional Development
- Partnership Agreement
- Mentor Professional Development Plan

Features

- Research based content in top ten areas of need for beginning teachers
- Ready to use materials
- Field tested content
- Identified supplemental materials available for additional support
- Aligns to daily needs and responsibilities of beginning teachers
- Sponge activities
- Celebration
- Content Related Reflection
- Extended Activities
- Journal Entries
- Participant Resources
- Embedded mentor self-analysis and goal setting related to mentoring practice

Benefits

- Research based
- Process based for immediate use and application
- Effective implementation strategies in any school setting
- Applicable in small to large school settings
- Complementary to any staff development program
- Align to foundational skills needed for mentoring
- Mentors apply knowledge and skills for professional growth
- Mentors align support to developmental needs of mentees
- Promotes reflective practice for continuous improvement
- Mentors develop system of evaluating their practice
- Teaching standards based

Acknowledgements

The authors wish to thank the following individuals:

Billie J. Enz, Associate Division Dean of Curriculum and Instruction/Professional Development Programs at Arizona State University. Thanks to Billie for having the vision to support all beginning educators, for starting the BEST program and for seeing our potential to bring leadership and ongoing development to BEST

Beth Lang, educator/staff developer, for her past research and initial contributions to curriculum development, choice activities, leadership and teaching in the BEST program.

Diana Jones, Administrative Assistant for the BEST Program, for assistance in formatting and typing drafts of the curriculum. We are grateful for her skills and support.

Karla Widger, *Yunn Lee*, *Beth Elmwood*, *Sarah Blaska* and *Gayle Molenaar* for their technical assistance.

The "original" *BEST Instructors*, for design team contribution for the Choice Activities.

BEST Cadre Instructors, who have taught the curriculum, implemented program components, and have provided instructor and beginning teacher feedback for ongoing program and material development.

Our Professional Mentors, who have modeled exemplar educator practices, encouraged and influenced our professional paths and will remain our valuable partners in education.

Educators everywhere who live the passion for impacting the learning and lives of children daily, hourly, moment-to-moment . . . We applaud your dedication to the profession and look forward with you to being advocates for teachers to promote the best for students and positively impact their success.

Dedication

The authors wish to thank our families, for their encouragement to our passion and vision for positively impacting the lives of students by supporting and developing great teachers.

Sharon would like to especially thank:

Karl, for your encouragement, your character and for knowing what really matters in life. Thanks for being the dad who brings laughter to the voices of our children and who sends everyone off with confidence for the day.

Kristen, whose love and smile are bright and whose character inspires me daily. Your insight into watching your teachers of today to become a teacher of tomorrow will impact your influence on the world.

Taylor, who when describing Mom's work says I "teach teachers how to teach teachers how to teach kids." It helps me know even on the days I work with the big people that I always have the heart for the little ones, too. You have a way of making everyone around you feel special. You make me proud.

And Jordan, who adds joy to all our days. Your love is energizing. I love you 25,000 times around the world and even more.

Dad and Mom, for building a legacy of love in our home and for our children. Thank you for being the most wonderful grandparents three children could dream for. Dad, I treasure your impact as an educator on my dedication to the field of education and my heart for valuing each individual student who we as educators serve.

Karla, for being the best "auntie," and being willing to have the footprints and fingerprints of my children in your home and on your heart.

Connie would like to especially thank:

Michael, my husband, for his constant support, always listening and encouraging me when I came to crossroads of career decisions. My professional growth has been nourished by his love.

Heather, my daughter and resident teacher. She developed the passion early. I wonder where that came from?

Kara, my daughter recently inspired to join the profession. My twin daughters have provided the diversions, laughter and motivation to balance the personal and professional endeavors.

James and Brayden, my grandsons, who continuously bring joy to my life.

In loving memory of Mom and Dad, who provided the love and care to my daughters and myself so I could fulfill my dream of growing in my profession. You inspired me to work hard and be happy. I am.

Introduction

The text has been created to provide resources and activities for support to you as a mentor educator.* It has been designed to help you grow in your professional support to the profession through the mentoring process. Each chapter contains:

- Content related information aligned to mentor development, needs of mentees and teaching standards
- Planning calendar
- Tips for success
- Checkpoints for mentoring opportunities aligned to school activities/responsibilities
- Topics to discuss with mentee
- Professional Development Lesson Plan to guide you through chapter content and activities
- Celebration
- Mentor/Mentee Interaction Logs
- Extended Choice Activities
- Journal Entry

The book has been formatted to support you in increasing your skills, providing meaningful reflection and setting goals for ongoing application. Embedded within the activities are opportunities for you to assess and showcase your growth as a mentor and the professional growth of your mentee. This process will reflect your professional journey as a mentor educator.

Take your time processing through the chapters. Think about and relate the content to your own mentoring practice. Gather additional on-site, in-district resources and ideas for personalized easy access. Create a system to organize collected materials and documents created. Take time to engage in the Choice Activities that will build your reflective practice and your practical application support to your mentee. Spend quality time with your mentee for insight and feedback in your role as mentor.

You will find through the mentoring process that you will be affirmed for the vast amount of knowledge and expertise you have as a seasoned teacher. Allow the mentoring process to inspire ongoing professional growth in your own teaching practice and renew your enthusiasm for being an advocate for teachers to gain competence in their role. Enjoy providing the inspiration to celebrate effective teaching practice, build effective teaching practice and strengthen our profession through your influence. The students will be the beneficiaries of your investment. Thank you!

*If the text is being used in alignment with developed seminar curriculum, you will receive direction for use of Participant Resources (labeled PR) from your seminar instructor.

> "Success is a journey, not a destination."
> —Ben Sweetland

Supplemental Resources

"The BEST Times" Newsletter

Eight newsletters aligned to beginning teacher and mentor teacher curriculum. Additional features include Resources and Administrator's Corner. Available through BEST program:

>BEST@asu.edu
>   or
>BEST
>Arizona State University
>College of Education
>P.O. Box 870211
>Tempe, AZ 85287-0211

* *Trade Secrets for Primary and Elementary Teachers*
by Billie J. Enz, Sharon A. Kortman, and Connie J. Honaker

* *Trade Secrets for Middle School and Secondary Teachers*
by Billie J. Enz, Connie J. Honaker, and Sharon A. Kortman

*Book available through Kendall/Hunt Publishing Company at www.kendallhunt.com

CHAPTER 1

Establishing the Mentoring Relationship

> "What lies behind us and what lies before us are tiny matters compared to what lies within us."
> —Oliver Wendell Holmes

Why mentoring?

Because mentoring . . .

- Builds best practices in teaching.
- Propels teacher effectiveness.
- Creates a collaborative community.
- Provides a guide on the side to fellow educators.
- Creates a process of continual self-reflection.
- Inspires life-long learning.
- Positively affects student success.
- Develops a renewed professional perspective for the mentor.
- Validates the mentor's knowledge and skills.
- Moves mentor to new role of teacher educator.

What is mentoring?

Mentoring is . . .

- Process of developing effective teaching practice.
- A collegial partnership.
- Self-analysis, reflection and application.
- Contributing to the standards of the profession.
- Development of new educators.
- Support of colleagues in multiple roles and responsibilities.
- A positive impact to the profession.
- A guide for defining practice.
- An equalizer in providing all students with the best educator possible.

Your role as a teacher leader is the most needed and influential element in developing and strengthening our profession. Research shows that the number one impact increasing teacher knowledge and skills is staff development. One-on-one mentoring provides the most focused and personalized professional growth opportunity.

New educators enter the profession with a high level of diversity in knowledge, skills and experiences. In addition, they are teaching a more diverse group of students. Consequently, the challenges facing the profession, including the mentors, create the intensified need for learning deliberate skills in mentoring and being able to tailor those skills to individual and site-based support. This support will also assist in minimizing teachers' feelings of isolation, a major reason they leave the profession yearly. Classroom doors open through mentoring, collaboration builds and the result is a coherent learning community. Let us begin . . .

Tip from Mentor Teacher

"There are so many things staff assumes new teachers know. Ask questions. Set your mentee up for success."

✓ POINTS

- ❏ Actively welcome colleague
- ❏ Mentor/mentee partnership agreement
- ❏ Plan regular meeting times with mentee
- ❏ Questions answered
- ❏ Back to school night
- ❏ First week's plan
- ❏ Management plan
- ❏ Sub folder

Month _____

Sunday	Monday	Tuesday	Wednesday	Thursday	Friday	Saturday

Topics to Discuss with Mentee

- ❏ Share ideas and materials for first day/week
- ❏ Procedures/routines for school site
- ❏ Mentor/mentee relationship expectations

COPYRIGHT © KENDALL/HUNT PUBLISHING COMPANY

Professional Development Lesson Plan

TIP: Welcome mentee.
Make regular visits to mentee's classroom.
Stay in close touch.

Subject _Establishing the Mentoring Relationship_   Class/Period _Seminar I_   Date _____

Objectives

- Understand the common needs of teachers.
- Know the typical five phases of beginning teachers and apply phases to the change process.
- Generate behaviors that build effective mentoring relationships.

Teaching Standard _Engages in Professional Development_

Set _Read introduction to chapter._

Procedures

1. Predict list of priority needs of teachers. Review <u>Top Ten Needs of New Teachers</u>. Compare to your prediction. Note your perception of differences based on beginning teachers, teachers new to district or assignment, veteran teachers and district or school-site considerations. Reflect on effectiveness of your role as mentor based on your understanding of your mentee's perceptions of need.

2. Read "The Stages of a Teacher's First Year" by Ellen Moir (PR1). Will facilitate understanding of year to come. Stages are highest in intensity to beginning educators, but are paralleled in the change process for anyone transitioning into a new or different role.

3. Review <u>Beginning Teacher Responses to Five Stages of First Year Teaching</u> (PR2). Use information to proactively provide timely support as needed for your mentee. Reminder: A mentor's support along with effective staff development opportunities are strong influences on helping a colleague adjust positively to his/her new position and accelerate professional growth.

4. Using PR3, <u>Behaviors of Effective Mentoring</u>, chart in the five topic areas provided, specific behaviors that create positive mentoring relationships. Contrasting with non-examples can help you clarify what behaviors you want to embrace in your own mentoring relationship.

5. Think of ways you can be an advocate for all beginning teachers based on knowledge learned. Apply to your mentoring relationship.

Closure/Self-Assessment/Reflection	Celebration!
❏ *Content Related Reflection* ❏ *Second Thoughts: Journal Reflection*	❏

Extended Activities

❏ *Mentor/Mentee Summary of Interaction*
❏ *Interactions Contact Log*
❏ *Choice Activities for Ongoing Professional Development*

Note:
Practice ←
↓
Reflect
↓
Document
↓
Apply →

Resources

❏ *Calendars** ❏ *Tip from Mentor Teacher*
❏ *Tip* ❏ *Topics to Discuss with Mentee*

*An additional calendar is added in this chapter to allow scheduling for additional months at the start of the school year.

Notes:

COPYRIGHT © KENDALL/HUNT PUBLISHING COMPANY

Top Ten Needs of New Teachers

- Classroom Management
- Student Motivation
- Individual Student Needs
- Student Assessment
- Classroom Organization
- Materials, Supplies and Additional Resources
- Lesson Planning
- Curriculum
- Relations with Parents
- Time Management

# ARTICLE

The Stages of a Teacher's First Year

— ELLEN MOIR —

To support new teachers effectively, other educators must understand the phases that novices often experience during their pivotal first year.

First-year teaching is a difficult challenge. Equally challenging is determining how to assist beginning teachers as they enter the profession. Since 1988, the Santa Cruz New Teacher Project, a 16-district consortium led by the University of California, Santa Cruz, has been supporting the efforts of new teachers. After working with nearly 1,500 new teachers, my colleagues and I have noted a number of developmental phases. Although not every new teacher goes through this exact sequence, understanding these phases is useful to educators who support new teachers, including administrators, teacher education faculty, and other support personnel.

New teachers move through several phases: from anticipation, to survival, to disillusionment, to rejuvenation, to reflection, then back to anticipation. Here's a look at the stages, exemplified by excerpts from new teachers' journal entries and end-of-the-year program evaluations.

Anticipation Phase

The anticipation phase begins during the student teaching portion of preservice preparation. The closer that student teachers get to completing their assignment, the more excited and anxious they become about their first teaching position. They tend to romanticize the role of the teacher. New teachers enter classrooms with a tremendous commitment to making a difference and a somewhat idealistic view of how to accomplish their goals. *"I was elated to get the job but terrified about going from the simulated experience of student teaching to being the person completely in charge."* This feeling of excitement carries new teachers through the first few weeks of school.

Survival Phase

The first month of school is overwhelming for new teachers. They are learning a lot at a rapid pace. Beginning teachers are bombarded with a variety of problems and situations they had not anticipated. Despite teacher education courses and student teaching experience, the realities of teaching on their own catch new teachers off guard. There is so little time and so much to learn. *"I thought I'd be busy—something like student teaching—but this is crazy. I'm constantly running. It's hard to focus on other aspects of my life."*

During the survival phase, most new teachers struggle to keep their heads above water. They become consumed with the day-to-day routine of teaching. It is not uncommon for new teachers to spend up to 70 hours a week on school work. They have little time to stop and reflect on their experiences.

Particularly overwhelming is the constant need to develop curriculum. Veteran teachers routinely reuse excellent lessons and units from past years. New teachers, still uncertain of what will really work, must develop their lessons for the first time. Even when they depend on textbooks and prepared curriculum, teaching unfamiliar content is enormously time-consuming.

"I thought there would be more time to get everything done. It's like working three jobs: 7:30–2:30, 2:30–6:00, with more time spent in the evening and on weekends." Although tired and surprised by the amount of work, first-year teachers usually maintain a tremendous amount of energy and commitment during the survival phase, and they harbor hope that soon the turmoil will subside.

Disillusionment Phase

After six to eight weeks of nonstop work and stress, new teachers enter the disillusionment phase. The intensity and the length of the phase vary among new teachers. The extensive time commitment, the realization that things are probably not going as smoothly as they would like, and low morale contribute to this period of disenchantment. New teachers begin questioning their commitment and their competence. Many new teachers fall ill during this phase.

Compounding an already difficult situation is the fact that new teachers confront several new events during this time frame: back-to-school night, parent conferences, and their first formal evaluation by the site administrator. Each milestone places an already vulnerable individual in a very stressful situation.

Back-to-school night means giving a speech to parents about plans for the year that are most likely still unclear in the new teacher's mind. Some parents are uneasy when they realize that the teacher is a beginner, and they may pose questions or make demands that intimidate a new teacher.

Copyright © 1999 by Ellen Moir. Reprinted by permission.

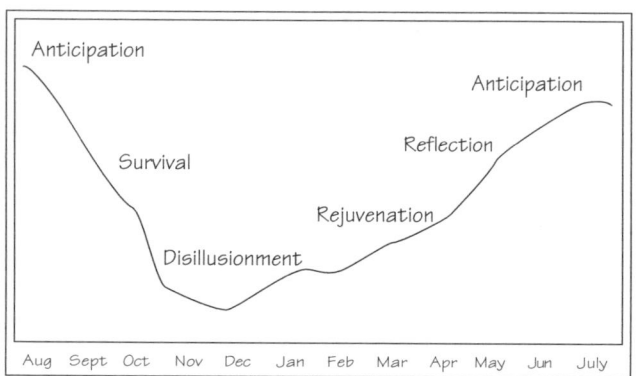

Figure 1: The Phases of a First-Year Teacher's Attitude Toward Teaching

Parent conferences require new teachers to be highly organized, articulate, tactful, and prepared to confer with parents about each student's progress. This type of communication with parents can be awkward and difficult for beginning teachers. New teachers generally begin with the idea that parents are partners in the learning process, and they are not prepared for parents' concerns or criticisms. These criticisms hit new teachers at a time of waning self-esteem.

This first formal evaluation by the principal also arrives during the disillusionment phase. Developing and presenting a "showpiece" lesson are time-consuming and stressful. New teachers, uncertain about the evaluation process and anxious about their own competence, question their ability to perform.

During the disillusionment phase, classroom management often becomes a major source of stress. *"I thought I'd be focusing more on curriculum and less on classroom management and discipline. I'm stressed because I have some very problematic students who are low academically, and I think about them every second my eyes are open."*

At this point, the accumulated stress on new teachers, coupled with months of overwork, provokes complaints from family members and friends. In the disillusionment phase, new teachers express self-doubt, have lower self-esteem, and question their professional commitment. Getting through this phase may be the toughest challenge they face as new teachers.

Rejuvenation Phase

The rejuvenation phase, which generally begins in January, is characterized by a slow improvement in the new teacher's attitude toward teaching. Having a winter break makes a tremendous difference for new teachers. The free time allows them to resume a more normal lifestyle, with plenty of rest, food, exercise, and time for family and friends. The break also offers an opportunity to organize materials and plan curriculum. This breathing space gives new teachers time for reflection and a chance to gain perspective. Most of all, it provides hope.

Putting past problems behind them, new teachers return to school rested and reinvigorated. They now have a better understanding of the system, more acceptance of the realities of teaching, and a sense of accomplishment at having made it through the first, and hardest, part of the school year. Although still months away, the end of school becomes a beacon of hope. By now, new teachers have also gained confidence and better coping skills to prevent or manage problems that they will encounter. During this phase, new teachers focus on curriculum development, long-term planning, and teaching strategies.

"I'm really excited about my story-writing center, although the organization of it has at times been haphazard. Story-writing has definitely revived my journals." The rejuvenation phase tends to last into spring, with many ups and downs along the way. Toward the end of this phase, new teachers begin to voice concerns about whether they can accomplish everything by the end of the school year. They also wonder how their students will perform on tests, once again questioning their own effectiveness as teachers. *"I'm fearful of these big tests. Can you be fired if your kids do poorly? I don't know enough about them to know what I haven't taught, and I'm sure it's a lot."*

Reflection Phase

The reflection phase begins during the last six weeks of school. These final weeks are a particularly invigorating time for first-year teachers. Reflecting back over the year, new teachers highlight events that were successful and those that were not. They think about the various changes that they plan to make the following year in management, curriculum, and teaching strategies. The end is in sight, and they have almost made it; but more important, a vision emerges about what their second year will look like, which brings them to a new phase of anticipation. *"I think that next year I'd like to start the letter puppets earlier to introduce the kids to more letters."*

It is essential that we assist new teachers and ease the transition from student teacher to full-time professional. Recognizing the phases that new teachers go through gives us a framework within which we can begin to design support programs to make the first year of teaching a more positive experience for our new colleagues.

END

Beginning Teacher Responses to Five Stages of First Year Teaching

Anticipation

Recommendations for Beginning Teacher	Recommendations for Mentor Teacher
• Talk to colleagues. • Observe other classroom environments/set-up. • Seek information/ask questions. • Tour school. • Get acquainted with neighboring classroom teachers. • Acquaint self with district curriculum guidelines. • Remember to balance priorities within the school day. • Establish and continue parent communication.	• Keep my hopes high. • Be extremely supportive. • Prepare me and give me an understanding of what is to come. • Share experiences to prepare me for what is coming. • Reinforce my efforts. • Listen to me. • Set up a specific time for us to meet on a regular basis.

Survival

Recommendations for Beginning Teacher	Recommendations for Mentor Teacher
• Prioritize and take one day at a time. • Prepare. Keep things in perspective. • Relax. • Focus on organizational skills which will help me be successful. • Realize the multitude of tasks and complexity of the job. • Go shopping for ideas. • Reflect on daily successes and keep on truckin'.	• Spend time with me. Make time for me. • Be available to assist with some of my "firsts," e.g. parent calls, grade level meetings, parent conference, etc. • Hand off a ready to use lesson and offer lesson suggestions! • Help me understand what I need to do and when to do it. • Check on my understanding of procedures and policies. • Listen to me. • Question me. • Stop by to talk and see how I am doing.

COPYRIGHT © KENDALL/HUNT PUBLISHING COMPANY

Disillusionment

Recommendations for Beginning Teacher	Recommendations for Mentor Teacher
• Remind myself I cannot do everything. • Use time wisely. • Take time out to exercise. • Communicate and share experiences with other beginning teachers; reflect and seek solutions. • Focus on the priorities. • Get to know my personal interests. • Listen to me. • Plan time to re-energize. • Design and implement engaging lessons plans. • Attend BEST seminar for encouragement and strategies to implement during this challenging stage.	• Tell me that you have "been there too;" share your experiences and solutions for difficult times. • Encourage me with kind words and actions. • When I get too frustrated, help me re-organize and begin again. • Be positive. Focus on the good. • Help me regroup and focus.

Rejuvenation

Recommendations for Beginning Teacher	Recommendations for Mentor Teacher
• Keep working hard and learning. • Spend time with family and friends. • Prioritize. • Be creative. Use resources. • Take time to reflect and learn from my experiences.	• Discuss upcoming activities and events. • Listen to me. • Have lunch together. • Challenge me to reflect and label my strengths. • Help me plan new goals for growth.

Reflection

Recommendations for Beginning Teacher	Recommendations for Mentor Teacher
• Document instructional strategies that worked. • Review the progress of my students. • Create list of the year's accomplishments. • Reflect and draft a professional goal for the upcoming year. • Set summer goals for preparation for the next school year. • Interact with other teachers and mentors.	• Celebrate me. • Continue journal sharing and e-mails. • Conference with me and help me summarize my school year.

Behaviors of Effective Mentoring

Building Trust

Example	Non-Example
Follow-through	Break commitment

Communicating Effectively

Example	Non-Example
Active listening	Always talking

Cultivating Confidence

Example	Non-Example
Providing positive feedback	General comments

Modeling Competence

Example	Non-Example
Model reflective practice	Only one way

Welcoming Colleague

Example	Non-Example
Schedule regular meeting times	"If you need me, my door is always open."

Content Related Reflection

How will information you learned today about the five phases assist you as you begin the school year with your mentee?

What is your greatest strength as you begin your mentoring?

What is your greatest challenge/fear as you begin your year of mentoring?

Mentor/Mentee Summary of Interaction*

Mentor Teacher Information
Name _____
District _____
School _____
Grade Level/Content Area _____

Mentee Teacher Information
Name _____
District _____
School _____
Grade Level/Content Area _____

Contact Information
Date of Contact _____
  Beginning Time _____
  Ending Time _____
  Total Time _____
Contact Initiated By
❏ Mentor Teacher ❏ Mentee Teacher

Type of Contact
❏ One-on-One   ❏ Drop-in Visit
❏ Journal   ❏ Classroom Observation
❏ Phone Call   ❏ Conference
❏ E-mail   ❏ Other _____

Questions/Issues to Address with Mentee:

Ideas Generated During Interaction:

Practical Applications:

*This form is to be duplicated as many times as needed. Create a section in your portfolio to file all interaction documentation.

COPYRIGHT © KENDALL/HUNT PUBLISHING COMPANY   Permission to duplicate for personal, non-commercial use.

Interactions Contact Log*

Date	Meeting Time	Total Time	Contact Initiated By Mentor Teacher or Mentee Teacher	Type of Contact One-on-One/Phone Call/ E-mail/Journal/Drop-in Visit/ Classroom Observation/ Conference/Other

*This form is to be duplicated as many times as needed. Create a section in your portfolio to file all interaction documentation.

Choice Activities for Ongoing Professional Development

CLASSROOM MANAGEMENT TIPS

Meet with another experienced teacher and generate a list of classroom management tips to give to your mentee. Share tips in the context of interacting with the new teacher and in relationship to his/her needs.

Build Reflective Practice
- Compose the list, summary of interaction with mentee and mentee's response to the tips.

COMMON QUESTIONS ASKED BY NEW TEACHERS

Meet with other experienced teachers and generate a list of common questions new teachers ask. Generate appropriate responses.

Build Reflective Practice
- Document list of questions and answers.

*Suggestion: Provide copy to administration for distribution to new staff and/or to mentors.

FRONT OFFICE INTERVIEW

Interview a building administrator or office employee to uncover the most frequently asked questions or misunderstandings from a new teacher.

Build Reflective Practice
- Include in summary your implementation mentoring plan from information gathered.

TIME MANAGEMENT TIPS

Reflect from your initial years of teaching to present, focusing on your successful time management tools. List at least ten tips. Share three or more with your mentee and give a copy of your list to other mentors at your site.

Build Reflective Practice
- Write a summary including a reflection from generating the list and responses to sharing the tips. Attach the list of time management tips.

Tip from Mentor Teacher

*"Use your sense of humor.
It opens the door for communication."*

- ❏ Build mentoring relationship
- ❏ Informal visit
- ❏ Note of encouragement
- ❏ Mentor interaction log
- ❏ Team plan parent teacher conferences
- ❏ Curriculum planning
- ❏ Grading system
- ❏ Kudo file

Month _____

Sunday	Monday	Tuesday	Wednesday	Thursday	Friday	Saturday

Topics to Discuss with Mentee

- ❏ Management concerns
- ❏ Communicating and working with parents
- ❏ Homework plans and ideas

Second Thoughts: Journal Reflection

"A teacher encourages tomorrow's dreams." —ANONYMOUS

CHAPTER 2

Encouraging Teachers through Mentoring

*"Tell me, I forget
Show me, I remember
Involve me, I understand."*

—Ancient Chinese Proverb

Mentoring is about helping a colleague self-identify strengths and areas of refinement for continual professional development. It is not about a veteran teacher creating a copy of him/herself or telling someone "how it should be done." Although the mentees will appreciate hearing an occasional story of your experience, they will grow faster when they can internalize or self identify areas of need and choices for decision making for continuous improvement. Your role as a mentor is to be a facilitator in that growth process.

Reflective questioning, specifically, provides a tool for mentors to guide communication for self-directed learning by the mentee. The process acknowledges the abilities and experiences of the mentee and provides a non-threatening path for guiding choices applicable to good teaching practice.

Understanding who we are and what motivates our thinking and behavior provides insight and is key to building the relationships necessary to promote personal and professional growth. Understanding your mentee will facilitate a process for specializing support based on mentee's personality and interaction style. In this chapter you will be introduced to different characteristics of personalities, typical stress responses and approaches to be successful in building a professional culture within your school. By valuing varying strengths of your colleagues, you can maximize communication. As a bonus, there is an effective transfer to the classroom and personal relationships which will encourage cooperative attitudes and behavior.

Relationships are enhanced through mentoring. Validating a person's style and personality enhances his/her ability to live positively. Reflective questioning is respectful and enhances self-reflection and effective mentoring practice. Gaining the insight and skills and deliberately implementing at appropriate times will continue to build teamwork, classroom practice, school improvement, systemic support, collegiality and parent/teacher communication. The interpersonal and technical skills applied will extend to the classroom, to the school site, to the district, and to the community to build a collaborative learning environment.

Tip from Mentor Teacher

"Begin conference time with reflective question. It promotes collegial dialogue."

✓ POINTS

- ❏ Plan visit to mentee's classroom
- ❏ Share the "good stuff" with colleagues/administration
- ❏ Assess mentee's needs
- ❏ Offer lesson suggestions
- ❏ Teacher evaluation
- ❏ Field trips
- ❏ Progress reports
- ❏ Always be positive!

Month _____

Sunday	Monday	Tuesday	Wednesday	Thursday	Friday	Saturday

Topics to Discuss with Mentee

- ❏ Extracurricular responsibilities
- ❏ Curriculum concerns
- ❏ Strategies for working with varied personalities

COPYRIGHT © KENDALL/HUNT PUBLISHING COMPANY

Professional Development Lesson Plan

TIP: *Provide a choice of meeting times with mentee.*

Subject _Encouraging Teachers through Mentoring_   Class/Period _Seminar 2_   Date _____

Objectives

- Examine and practice the art of reflective questioning.
- Identify interaction styles in relationship to mentoring practice.
- Understand four Personal Objectives.
- Self-analyze and generate a proactive mentoring action plan.

Teaching Standard _Engages in Professional Development_

Set _Read introduction to chapter._

Procedures

1. Write a _Celebration_ (PR4) of your new mentoring experience. Celebrate your new role!

2. Preview _Reflective Summary Guide_ (PR6). As you read "Using Reflective Questioning To Promote Collaborative Dialogue" (PR5), complete the guide.

3. Utilizing _Reflective Questioning Role-Play_ (PR7) practice reflective questioning techniques with colleagues. Apply questioning strategy to mentoring relationship as appropriate.

4. Complete _Array Interaction Inventory_.

5. Read "The Array Interaction Model" information. Use _Array Interaction Model Guide_ (PR8) to record Personal Objective characteristics.

6. Using _Array Interaction Model Guide_ (PR8), complete _Array Proactive Mentoring Plan_ (PR9) for implementation to mentoring partnership.

7. Have your mentee complete _Array Interaction Inventory_ (PR10). Share information learned about the model. Discuss the benefits with your mentee to working together.

Closure/Self-Assessment/Reflection	Celebration!
❑ *Content Related Reflection* ❑ *Second Thoughts: Journal Reflection*	❑ *Celebration (PR4)*

Extended Activities

❑ *Mentor/Mentee Summary of Interaction*
❑ *Interactions Contact Log*
❑ *Choice Activities for Ongoing Professional Development*

Note:
Practice ←
↓
Reflect
↓
Document
↓
Apply ─┘

Resources

❑ *Calendar*   ❑ *Tip from Mentor Teacher*
❑ *Tip*   ❑ *Topics to Discuss with Mentee*

Notes:

Celebration

Using Reflective Questioning to Promote Collaborative Dialogue

GINNY V. LEE
BRUCE G. BARNETT

Reflective questioning creates opportunities for individuals to reflect aloud, to be heard by one or more colleagues, and to be prompted to expand and extend thinking through follow-up questions.

For some time now, reflective practice has occupied a position of importance in the professions (Schön, 1983). Its relevance for educators today is heightened by the current focus on the development of learning communities and learning organizations (Senge, 1990). Reflection is essential to educators' capacity to think not only about their practice but also about *how* they think, their implicit theories, and the sense they make of their experiences (Argyris & Schön, 1975). The experience of reflection is enhanced when professionals are able to communicate with each other in ways that encourage and expand the process.

The use of reflection and reflective practices as strategies for developing more thoughtful and effective educators raises a number of important questions for staff developers. What kinds of activities and programs should be implemented to establish habits of reflection among prospective and practicing school personnel? How does a staff developer encourage and support reflection in professional development settings? How does a district or site administrator provide opportunities for reflection among colleagues?

One powerful form of reflection occurs when educators engage in professional dialogue with each other in small groups. The value of such professional exchanges is enhanced when participants use specific questioning skills to support the reflective process. *Reflective questioning* creates opportunities for individuals to reflect aloud to be heard by one or more colleagues, and to be prompted to expand and extend thinking through follow-up questions. Reflective questioning is a skill that can be developed and used by educators in all roles. Individuals can use it with peers, clients, supervisees, students (adult or youth), interns or mentees, and so forth.

This article is based on our experiences over the past decade teaching reflective questioning skills to educators and staff developers in the United States, Canada, Australia, and Europe. It includes background information about the origin of the strategy, describes various forms of reflective questioning and conditions that support its use, and provides guidelines for formulating and asking reflective questions. We provide two anecdotes to suggest the kinds of outcomes that can be reached through this strategy and conclude with recommendations to staff developers.

Origin of Reflective Questioning

The source of the reflective questioning strategy is the qualitative research methodology used by staff of the Far West Laboratory for Educational Research and Development (FWL) in its intensive study of school administrators (Dwyer et al., 1985). Participants reported that the process of being observed and interviewed about their work provided them with valuable opportunities for reflection and self-assessment (Dwyer et al., 1983). This, in turn, led FWL staff to create a program of professional development that encouraged school leaders to work with each other in a similar fashion.

In the Peer-Assisted Leadership (PAL) program, school leaders work with peer colleagues to engage in inquiry, reflection, and analysis about their own work. Partners learn specific skills that they use to observe and interview each other on the job over time, collecting and analyzing information about their own and their partners' leadership activities. The process can be likened both to action research and peer coaching. (Complete descriptions of PAL appear in Barnett, 1989, and Lee, 1991.)

In PAL, the basic building blocks of the inquiry process are shadowing and reflective interviewing. Shadowing creates a record of an administrator's work activities through direct observation: the reflective interview is used to extend the learning after the observation. By asking questions about the observation, the interviewer provides an opportunity for his or her partner to reflect on what occurred. These reflections may include thoughts about how and why events unfolded, feeling associated with events, exploration of alternatives, plans for next steps, and so forth.

By thinking about the events, the observed person achieves a greater awareness of self and an increased understanding of

---

From *Journal of Staff Development*, Winter 1994, Vol. 15, No. 1 by Ginny V. Lee & Bruce G. Barnett. Copyright 1994 by National Staff Development Council. Reprinted by permission.

how he or she enacts the role of school leader. This awareness and understanding encompasses areas such as personal and professional values and priorities, theoretical and applied knowledge, preferred modes of action, and the strengths and limitations one brings to the leadership task. As participants carry out multiple cycles of observation and interviewing, they are able to examine how policies, practices, and resources are linked as a system in their school (Barnett, 1990).

Reflection is also used in professional development activities such as coaching and mentoring in which the goal is to provide participants with a process of peer dialogue about their educational practice. We use the term "reflective interview" to describe the process when reflection is coupled with a shadowing experience. But direct observation is not a prerequisite to a reflective interaction, in which case we use the term "reflective questioning" to describe the interaction process.

Developing Reflective Questioning Skills

Reflective questioning is a technique in which one person prepares and asks questions that are designed to provide opportunities for the respondent to explore his or her knowledge, skills, experiences, attitudes, beliefs, and values. In a professional development setting, the typical goal is to broaden and deepen the respondent's understanding with respect to self, work roles, and/or performance.

Reflective questioning encourages the respondent to explore his or her *own* thinking: it is not intended to direct the respondent to a conclusion pre-determined by the questioner. For questioning to be truly reflective, the questioner must respect the respondent's statements, suspend judgment, and avoid attempts to manipulate his or her thinking.

When is Reflective Questioning Appropriate?

To determine if the strategy might be beneficial, the questioner must consider the context in which it will be used, the purpose for its use, and the relationship between himself or herself and the person(s) being questioned.

Context and purpose. Any context that calls for thoughtful and personal consideration invites reflective questioning. Processes may include considering alternative courses of action, examining relations between desired and achieved outcomes, clarifying beliefs or values, exploring commonalities (such as shared experiences, challenges, beliefs) within a group, reviewing the significance of an experience, and so forth.

Reflective questioning is appropriate only if its purpose is to support the respondent(s) in a *personalized process of exploration*. The questioner must be willing and able to work with whatever ideas, information, thoughts, and feelings arise. In contrast, the questioning process loses its reflective quality when the questioning is designed to lead the respondent to see what the questioner wants him or her to see, or to assess or evaluate the response.

Relationship with the respondent. The questioner's professional (and perhaps personal) relationship to the respondent influences the questioning process, as does the way the questioner treats the information received. For example, a supervisor may find that the best opportunities for reflective questioning are at times other than when he or she is engaged in evaluation of the other person's performance, since the evaluation process requires making judgments, which will hinder the reflective dialogue.

What Type of Climate Supports Reflective Questioning?

Before one can change something it is necessary to know what is occurring now. The change process often begins with increased self awareness and a willingness to examine one's own current practice. Even when the purpose of a reflective activity is simply increasing awareness of self, the process involves some risk. Thus, a climate of trust is important for supporting the process.

Questioners can help achieve such a climate by establishing two important norms: confidentiality and a non-judgmental stance in the interaction. These norms apply not only to the interaction between two individuals, but also among the members of larger groups that are engaged in reflective questioning. Group facilitators need to make these norms explicit and hold group members accountable for them. When participants find that revealing their thoughts and feelings can be done without fear of judgment or censure, they are able to process questions in greater depth.

Preparing and Asking Reflective Questions

Our experience has shown that most educators need assistance in learning to create reflective questions and in assessing how their verbal and non-verbal behaviors can promote reflective dialogue. We provide guidelines for preparing and asking questions and have educators practice these skills with each other. The guidelines are summarized in Figure 1 and described in the following sections.

The practice activities involve multiple opportunities to create and ask reflective questions in groups of two or three. These questions are typically based on role plays and participants' recollections of their own experiences. Written vignettes, case studies, and videotaped segments can also serve as the sources

Preparing Questions	Asking Questions
1. Base questions on the respondent's own experiences.	1. Use a neutral tone of voice.
2. Word questions in neutral, non-judgmental ways.	2. Incorporate active listening skills.
3. Keep an overall purpose in mind.	3. Refrain from giving advice.
4. Be prepared to follow up initial questions.	

Figure 1: Guidelines for Preparing and Asking Reflective Questions

of situations for reflective questioning practice. Participants receive feedback on their practice activities from each other and from the workshop facilitator. As repeated practice cycles are carried out, participants are regularly asked to step back from the experience to reflect on what they are learning, which in turn supports them in refining and expanding their skills.

Preparing questions. The following four guidelines help questioners prepare questions.

1. *Base questions on the respondent's own experiences.* For questions to encourage a respondent to reflect, they must make sense to the person. When people reflect, they are exploring their own experiences. Individuals can reflect on others' experiences only in reference to themselves. For example, a person compares a colleague's experience to his or her own or reaches his or her own interpretation of its meaning. Questions need to be anchored in the experiences of the person being questioned if they are to be perceived as authentic.
2. *Word questions in neutral, non-judgmental ways.* Questions that use loaded language will be more likely to inhibit the reflective process than to support it. Questions should avoid implying that the questioner has the correct answer, expects an appropriate response, or is engaged in assessment or evaluation. For example, interviewers should avoid using phrases such as, "Why didn't you. . . .?", "Don't you think that. . .?" or "Weren't you really trying to . . .?".
3. *Keep an overall purpose in mind.* Again, for questions to make sense to individuals, there needs to be some reason for the questioner to be asking them, some purpose for the interaction. Reflective questions can assist during the early stages of forming a professional relationship and later as part of self-assessment and in planning future actions. There is no single "right purpose" for reflective questioning. To be useful to participants, however, the exchange should have some purpose about which the participants are in accord.
4. *Be prepared to follow up initial questions.* A reflective dialogue develops through interaction. The initial question may open the door to reflection, but the process will not be sustained unless the questioner is prepared to go the next step. This means having follow-up questions in mind and adjusting the succeeding questions in response to what the respondent is saying.

Reflective questioning can be compared to a dance in which the questioner both leads and follows. While he or she has a purpose in mind and a sense of where the dialogue may go, the questioner also follows the respondent's direction and takes cues about follow-up questions based on what is said.

Asking questions. Once questions are prepared, three additional guidelines will assist questioners in the reflective dialogue.

1. *Use a neutral tone of voice.* Intonation and body language need to be congruent with the non-judgmental words to deliver a supportive message. A phrase such as "Can you explain what you mean by that?" becomes highly charged if the emphasis is placed on the word "explain," "mean," or "that," of if one's posture becomes aggressive.
2. *Incorporate active listening skills.* The reflective process can be assisted by allowing the respondent ample time and opportunity to think aloud and to expand on initial thoughts. Active listening includes such skills as making eye contact, nodding, restating key words, and including sounds that signal the respondent to continue (for example, "uh-huh" or "mm-hm"). The questioner should not be so eager to go on to the next question that he or she cuts off the respondent's thinking.
3. *Refrain from giving advice.* Providing advice shifts the dialogue away from reflection to problem solving. The respondent may welcome (or even ask for) advice, but the questioner's opinions can influence the direction and content of reflection away from the respondent's own thinking. We recommend that problem solving and advice giving be kept separate from reflective dialogue.

What Types of Questions Promote Reflection?

As we work with groups of educators to develop reflective questioning skills, we frequently encounter the belief that meaning-

EXAMPLE	CONSEQUENCE/REACTION
Clarifying Questions	
Tell me about how your reading program is organized and delivered.	Allows respondent to describe a situation in his/her own words
What happened when you spoke with the parents?	Encourages respondent to provide detailed information
Purpose/Consequence Questions	
What kinds of outcomes do you anticipate occurring if the teachers start the program?	Recognizes the possible results associated with an event
What reason guided your choosing these children to participate in the program?	Allows respondent to indicate the rationale for his or her decision
Linking Questions	
You indicated that many students have low self-esteem. You also mentioned that a new program you've started is aimed at social responsibility. Is there a relationship between these two issues?	Encourages respondent to tie together different pieces of information
How has this experience validated or changed your thinking?	Acknowledges how experiences influence respondent's attitudes and behaviors

Figure 2: Types of Questions and Statements That Can Encourage Reflection

ful reflection will occur only if the "right" questions are asked. We have found this not to be the case. Rather, we find that some very basic and even obvious types of questions are helpful. Simply saying. "Tell me more about that situation" or "Can you give me an example?" will stimulate reflection.

Our experience has taught us that the attitudes and behavior of the questioner are at least as important as the questions he or she asks. Attitudes that facilitate reflection demonstrating genuine interest in what the other has to say, listening attentively to responses and building from them in the dialogue, and supporting the other person in speaking authentically and honestly. In addition, we have found that there are some general types of questions that facilitate the reflective process. Figure 2 provides examples of the three types of questions described below.

Clarifying questions. These questions provide an opportunity for the respondent to clarify events, actions, feelings, thoughts, or beliefs. Questions that allow a person to describe a situation, for example, serve at least three functions: they anchor reflection in the concrete reality of experience; they provide an opportunity for the person to recapture the event for purposes of examination; and they serve as a springboard for deeper exploration of meanings, alternatives, and conclusions.

Thus, while it might seem that clarifying questions are "pre-reflective," they are often an essential part of the reflective process. Question stems for clarifying questions include: "How would you describe . . ."; "Can you recall what occurred . . ."; What happened when you . . ." The basic "who," "what," "when," and "where" questions asked by newspaper reporters can serve as the start of clarifying questions.

Purpose and consequence questions. Questions that allow individuals to consider both the intended and unintended outcomes of situations assist them in seeing cause and effect relationships connected to their own actions. This is a stepping stone to considering if these are the individual's desired outcomes which, in turn, may lead to change. Question stems for this type of question might be: "What were you hoping to accomplish by . . ."; "What kinds of outcomes did you anticipate . . ."; "What reasons guided your choice of . . .". This type of question is often inquiring about the "why" aspect of the respondent's behavior or thinking without directly saying, "Why did you do that?".

Linking questions. One of the most important uses of reflective questioning is to support educators in articulating the connections among various elements of their professional worlds. When educators can explore their own implicit theories of action, they are in a much stronger position to consider changes in their behavior (Argyris & Schön, 1975; Osterman & Kottkamp, 1993).

Linking questions provide opportunities for respondents to consider relationships among variables such as the specific contexts in which they act, their own personal/professional histories, their beliefs and values, their goals and aspirations, the resources available to them, their interdependence with other professionals, their interpersonal relationships, and the knowledge and skills base that guide them. Questions that encourage linking will often take the form of mirroring back two or more ideas or pieces of information from the respondent's previous responses and asking if they might be related.

Linking questions need to be open enough for the respondent to reflect on the basis of his or her own experiences, as opposed to what the person may think should be the answer. A question to elicit a teacher's thinking about instructional strategies and student learning, for example, must communicate permission to consider how his or her actual experience may not match what was taught during preservice or inservice activities.

Another type of linking question is the "So what?" question. This type of question is often used at the conclusion of a workshop when a facilitator asks participants to consider the implications of the experience for them as they anticipate returning to the workplace. Similarly, when an administrator reviews with a staff member a particularly challenging situation and its eventual outcome, this kind of question can assist him or her in generalizing from the experience.

Outcomes Associated with Reflective Questioning

Our experience suggests there are multiple benefits for educators who work closely with their peers in creating and asking reflective questions. Not only do they gain new insights and knowledge by reflecting on their own situations, but they also benefit by suspending judgment in attempting to better understand the context, rationale, and consequences of other professionals' situations (Barnett, 1990; Lee, 1991). Two anecdotes illustrate the types of effects we have observed.

A common outcome is that an individual's thinking and action are influenced during the reflective questioning process. A prime illustration of this occurred after a principal had observed a colleague conducting a teacher evaluation session. Before engaging the colleague in the reflective questioning process, he was quite skeptical about the way in which she had conducted the evaluation and questioned the appropriateness of her approach. Nevertheless, he assumed a neutral and non-judgmental position, setting aside his interpretation while he used reflective questions to explore the situation.

His colleague clarified the background of her school's teacher evaluation system, explained her reasons for using it, and described its effect on teachers. As a result, he found himself not only understanding her perspective but also shifting his own beliefs. He ultimately decided to incorporate some of his colleague's ideas into his own teacher evaluations.

Reflective questioning also has an effect on educators' *collective* actions (Mueller & Lee, 1989). A group of administrators participated in the year-long PAL process. As a result of the trust, mutual respect, and shared understanding that developed among participants, the group decided to continue meeting to discuss and resolve common problems they faced.

Initially, the group addressed curricular and instructional challenges in their individual schools. Further reflection led them to a district wide problem. They were called away from their sites several times each September for district meetings, detracting from getting the school year underway efficiently. The group approached central office personnel who, upon realizing the dilemma they were creating, changed the district's calendar to avoid September meetings. Based on their initial success in working collaboratively with district officials, the group took on additional district wide improvement efforts, such as developing an alternative evaluation procedure for principals. The group became a significant part of the district's decision making process.

Conclusions and Recommendations

For educators who are learning the strategy of reflective questioning, especially for those in positions of leadership and authority, one of the greatest challenges is the suspension of judgment. Staff developers who are accustomed to providing expert answers might also find it difficult to acquire and demonstrate the reflective questioning strategy. The following guidelines can help.

1. *Recognize and honor the importance of hearing and being heard.* We all know what it feels like when we are speaking to someone who presumes to know what we think before we say it, or doesn't really hear/understand what we mean, or passes judgment without knowing the whole story. It can be both frustrating and demeaning.

   The same is true in the reflective questioning process. The questioner must acknowledge and remember that she or he really cannot know how another person sees things or why another person acted in a certain way without first hearing that person speak. All of us believe we have good reasons to think and act as we do. As reflective questioners, we must remember that our colleagues believe the same of themselves.

2. *Keep the process at the forefront.* The success of reflective questioning does not depend on asking "just the right question." It relies much more on creating opportunities for respondents to think aloud and construct meaning for themselves. The questioner needs to focus more on whether the process is providing such opportunities than whether particular questions are being asked.

When staff developers and other educational leaders can assist colleagues in learning ways of talking together that increase understanding of self and others, the stage is being set for collaborative dialogues about improving collective practice. Reflective questioning is a promising strategy in the creation of such learning communities within and across schools.

References

Argyris, C., & Schön, D.A. (1975). *Theory in practice: Increasing professional effectiveness.* San Francisco: Jossey-Bass.

Barnett, B.G. (1989). Using peer observation and feedback to reduce principals' isolation. *Journal of Educational Administration, 27*(2), 46–56.

Barnett, B.G. (1990). Peer-assisted leadership: Expanding principals' knowledge through reflective practice. *Journal of Educational Administration, 28*(3), 67–76.

Dwyer, D.C., Lee, G.V., Rowan, B., & Bossert, S.T. (1983). *Five principals in action: Perspectives on instructional management.* San Francisco: Far West Laboratory for Educational Research and Development.

Dwyer, D.C., Lee, G.V., Barnett, B.G., Filby, N.N., & Rowan, B. (1985). *Understanding the principal's contribution to instruction: Seven principals, seven stories.* San Francisco: Far West Laboratory for Educational Research and Development.

Lee, G.V. (1991, Spring). Peer-assisted development of school leaders. *Journal of Staff Development, 12*(2), 14–18.

Mueller, F.L., & Lee, G.V. (1989). Changes abound when peers become PALs. *The School Administrator, 46*(2), 16–18.

Osterman, K.F., & Kottkamp, R.B. (1993). *Reflective practice for educators: Improving schooling through professional development.* Newbury Park, CA: Corwin Press.

Schön, D.A. (1983). *The reflective practitioner.* New York: Basic Books.

Senge, P.M. (1990). *The fifth disciple: The art and practice of the learning organization.* New York: Doubleday/Currency.

END

Reflective Summary Guide

What is Reflective Questioning?

Examples of Reflective Questions

Non-Examples of Reflective Questions

Article Response

Reflective Questioning Role-Play

Role Responsibilities

Mentee: Describe your challenge (listed below) to your mentor.

Mentor: Practice reflective questioning using *Reflective Questioning Guide* for examples. Your goal is to assist your mentee in processing his/her thinking and choice of strategies.

Recorder: Script the responses of the mentor. Make note of any nonverbal behaviors that you observe.

Rotate roles for each challenge.

Challenge One

New Colleague is upset about a letter received from a parent.

Mentor Verbal Responses	Nonverbal Mentor Behaviors

Reflection

Challenge Two

New Colleague has several students in one class exhibiting negative behaviors.

Mentor Verbal Responses	Nonverbal Mentor Behaviors

Reflection

Challenge Three

New Colleague is feeling overwhelmed by teaching responsibilities.

Mentor Verbal Responses	Nonverbal Mentor Behaviors

Reflection

Array Interaction Inventory

Complete the following survey to help identify your primary and secondary personal objectives, the most natural way you tend to respond to the world based on your personality.

Directions:
- Rank order the responses in rows below on a scale from 1 to 4 with <u>1</u> being "<u>least</u> like me" to <u>4</u> being "<u>most</u> like me."
- After you have ranked each row, add down each column.
- The column(s) with the highest score(s) shows your primary Personal Objective(s) in your personality.

In your normal day-to-day life, you tend to be:			
Nurturing / Sensitive / Caring	Logical / Systematic / Organized	Spontaneous / Creative / Playful	Quiet / Insightful / Reflective

In your normal day-to-day life, you tend to value:			
Harmony / Relationships are important	Work / Time schedules are important	Stimulation / Having fun is important	Reflection / Having some time alone is important

In most settings, you are usually:			
Authentic / Compassionate / Harmonious	Traditional / Responsible / Parental	Active / Opportunistic / Spontaneous	Inventive / Competent / Seeking

In most situations, you could be described as:			
Empathetic / Communicative / Devoted	Practical / Competitive / Loyal	Impetuous / Impactful / Daring	Conceptual / Knowledgeable / Composed

You approach most tasks in a(n) _____ manner.			
Affectionate / Inspirational / Vivacious	Conventional / Orderly / Concerned	Courageous / Adventurous / Impulsive	Rational / Philosophical / Complex

When things start to "not go your way" and you are tired and worn down, what might your responses be?			
Say "I'm sorry" / Make mistakes / Feel badly	Over-control / Become critical / Take charge	"It's not my fault" / Manipulate / Act out	Withdraw / Don't talk / Become indecisive

When you've "had-a-bad-day" and you become frustrated, how might you respond?			
Over-please / Cry / Feel depressed	Be perfectionistic / Verbally attack / Overwork	Become physical / Be irresponsible / Demand attention	Disengage / Delay / Daydream

Add score:							
	Harmony		Production		Connection		Status Quo

© Kortman, 1997

COPYRIGHT © KENDALL/HUNT PUBLISHING COMPANY

Personal Objectives/Personality Components

Teacher and student personalities are a critical element in the classroom dynamic. The Array Interaction Model identifies four personality components called "Personal Objectives." All people have all four components; however, one or two are more prominent and tend to greatly influence the way a person sees the world and responds to it. A person whose primary Personal Objective is Harmony is feeling-oriented, and is caring and sensitive. A person with a primary Personal Objective of Production is organized, logical and thinking-oriented. A person whose primary Personal Objective is Connection is enthusiastic, spontaneous and action-oriented. A person whose primary Personal Objective is Status Quo is insightful, reflective and observant. The following figure presents the Array Model descriptors, offers specific Cooperative and Reluctant behaviors from each Personal Objective, and addresses needs associated with each in a classroom setting.

Array Interaction Model

	Personal Objectives/Personality Component			
	HARMONY	PRODUCTION	CONNECTION	STATUS QUO
COOPERATIVE (Positive Behavior)	Caring Sensitive Nurturing Harmonizing	Logical Structured Organized Systematic	Spontaneous Creative Playful Enthusiastic	Quiet Imaginative Insightful Reflective
PRIMARY WAY OF VIEWING THE WORLD	Feeling	Thinking	Action	Observation
RELUCTANT (Negative Behavior)	Overadaptive Overpleasing Makes mistakes Cries or giggles Self-defeating	Overcritical Overworks Perfectionist Verbally attacks Demanding	Disruptive Blames Irresponsible Demands attention Defiant	Disengaging Withdrawn Delays Despondent Daydreams
PSYCHOLOGICAL NEEDS	Friendships Sensory experience	Task completion Time schedule	Contact with people Fun activities	Alone time Stability
WAYS TO MEET NEEDS	Value their feelings Comfortable work place Pleasing learning environment Cozy corner	Value their ideas Incentives Rewards Leadership positions Schedules To-do lists	Value their activity Hands-on activities Group interaction Games Change in routine	Value their privacy Alone time Independent activities Specific directions Computer activities Routine tasks

Teacher Scenarios

HARMONY

Bob's response on the "I Know Me" survey indicates he rates high in the Harmony Personal Objective. When in a normal state (cooperative), he is caring and pro-social. His relationships with his students, and with family and friends, are important to him. He enjoys the school community and feels privileged to be impacting the lives of his students.

When highly stressed, Bob tends to over-adapt, over-please and make mistakes on the most routine items.

Bob tends to be stressed by large amounts of paperwork, lack of social time with colleagues and not enough time to have one-on-one interactions with students. He may procrastinate, waste time by socializing and then feel badly because he doesn't have time for family, friends, or tasks that must be completed. He has a poor filing system, which expounds his paper dilemma. He also has a difficult time saying "no" and frequently finds himself on numerous committees and planning teams with a schedule that is overwhelming.

PRODUCTION

Mia's survey indicates she has a Production Personal Objective. She is logical, structured, organized and persistent. She is a thinker, a problem solver, likes information exchange and values such things as using time efficiently, task completion, skill development, and schedules. Mia has many ideas and enjoys sharing them with colleagues. She is efficient, and her desk, lesson plans and materials are always well organized.

When Mia is stressed, she may become critical of herself and others. She may verbally disagree with a colleague's actions. She may put undue pressure on herself to do things perfectly, even neglecting to eat in order to finish a task.

She is most likely to become stressed by too many unnecessary meetings, changes in scheduling and job descriptions, interruptions, or lack of specific information. She tends to become curt when colleagues "waste her time" by engaging in frivolous chatter when she knows she could be accomplishing other more relevant tasks with her valuable time.

CONNECTION

Billie rated herself as having a Connection Personal Objective. She loves activity and action and enters a room with energy. She is friendly and bright eyed, connects with others in positive ways, enjoys music and drama and is very creative. She likes to try new things and never teaches the same material the same way twice. She enjoys the spontaneous moment.

When stressed, Billie can become irresponsible, disruptive, attention-getting and blaming. Her jokes may become inappropriate and sarcastic. She can become openly defiant to authority.

Billie is stressed by high levels of structure, and when there is no room for creative thought or spontaneity in her planning or teaching, she stresses with relentless meetings, inflexible time schedules, and too much paperwork.

STATUS QUO

Jose's survey results identify Status Quo as his Personal Objective. Jose is very quiet and reserved, insightful and reflective. When he speaks, both colleagues and students listen. He is good at repetitive tasks and enjoys putting lessons together on the computer and finding out additional information and activities from resources on the internet.

When Jose becomes stressed, he begins to withdraw. He may lack enthusiasm and demonstrates little effort. He allows the students to do their own thing and doesn't pull it all back together for closure. He may sit at his desk to grade papers and find that 20 minutes has elapsed as he has been in a blank stare.

Jose is most likely to be stressed by lack of specific direction and insufficient information. He is also stressed by too much activity with no break time for regrouping his thoughts and feelings. He tends to waste time by withdrawing and becoming indecisive.

Adapted from *Trade Secrets*, 1999.

Array Interaction Model Guide

Interaction Styles

- *Cooperative*—positive, agreeable, helpful and collaborative behaviors
- *Marginal*—neutral in attitudes and disengaged in interactions
- *Reluctant*—involved in negative behaviors

Personal Objectives

Harmony

Cooperative
- caring

| feeling |

Reluctant
- over-pleasing

Production

Cooperative
- logical

| thinking |

Reluctant
- demanding

Connection

Cooperative
- creative

| action |

Reluctant
- disruptive

Status Quo

Cooperative
- quiet

| observation |

Reluctant
- withdrawn

PR8

Array Proactive Mentoring Plan

Directions
From the Array Proactive Mentoring Charts, identify one mentoring behavior for each Personal Objective that you will implement for your mentoring action plan.

Personal Objectives

Harmony	**Production**
Example: I will write notes of encouragement.	Example: I will plan ahead for mentee conferences.
Connection	**Status Quo**
Example: I will provide a variety of choices for our contacts.	Example: I will establish a reflective communication tool.

PR9

Array Interaction Inventory

Directions:
- Rank order the responses in rows below on a scale from 1 to 4 with **1** being "<u>least</u> like me" to **4** being "<u>most</u> like me."
- After you have ranked each row, add down each column.
- The column(s) with the highest score(s) shows your primary Personal Objective(s) in your personality.

In your normal day-to-day life, you tend to be:			
Nurturing Sensitive Caring	Logical Systematic Organized	Spontaneous Creative Playful	Quiet Insightful Reflective
In your normal day-to-day life, you tend to value:			
Harmony Relationships are important	Work Time schedules are important	Stimulation Having fun is important	Reflection Having some time alone is important
In most settings, you are usually:			
Authentic Compassionate Harmonious	Traditional Responsible Parental	Active Opportunistic Spontaneous	Inventive Competent Seeking
In most situations, you could be described as:			
Empathetic Communicative Devoted	Practical Competitive Loyal	Impetuous Impactful Daring	Conceptual Knowledgeable Composed
You approach most tasks in a(n) _____ manner.			
Affectionate Inspirational Vivacious	Conventional Orderly Concerned	Courageous Adventurous Impulsive	Rational Philosophical Complex
When things start to "not go your way" and you are tired and worn down, what might your responses be?			
Say "I'm sorry" Make mistakes Feel badly	Over-control Become critical Take charge	"It's not my fault" Manipulate Act out	Withdraw Don't talk Become indecisive
When you've "had-a-bad-day" and you become frustrated, how might you respond?			
Over-please Cry Feel depressed	Be perfectionistic Verbally attack Overwork	Become physical Be irresponsible Demand attention	Disengage Delay Daydream
Add score:			
Harmony	Production	Connection	Status Quo

© Kortman, 1997

PR10

Content Related Reflection

Based on your experiences and learning today in the areas of reflective questioning and the Array Interaction Model, what skills are now available to you as you become a teacher educator?

Mentor/Mentee Summary of Interaction*

Mentor Teacher Information
Name _____
District _____
School _____
Grade Level/Content Area _____

Mentee Teacher Information
Name _____
District _____
School _____
Grade Level/Content Area _____

Contact Information
Date of Contact _____
   Beginning Time _____
   Ending Time _____
   Total Time _____

Contact Initiated By
❏ Mentor Teacher   ❏ Mentee Teacher

Type of Contact
❏ One-on-One   ❏ Drop-in Visit
❏ Journal   ❏ Classroom Observation
❏ Phone Call   ❏ Conference
❏ E-mail   ❏ Other _____

Questions/Issues to Address with Mentee:

Ideas Generated During Interaction:

Practical Applications:

*This form is to be duplicated as many times as needed. Create a section in your portfolio to file all interaction documentation.

Permission to duplicate for personal, non-commercial use.   COPYRIGHT © KENDALL/HUNT PUBLISHING COMPANY

Interactions Contact Log*

Date	Meeting Time	Total Time	Contact Initiated By Mentor Teacher or Mentee Teacher	Type of Contact One-on-One/Phone Call/ E-mail/Journal/Drop-in Visit/ Classroom Observation/ Conference/Other

*This form is to be duplicated as many times as needed. Create a section in your portfolio to file all interaction documentation.

Choice Activities for Ongoing Professional Development

TIPS FOR WRITTEN COMMUNICATION TO PARENTS

Review samples of your written communication to parents with your mentee. Proofread and edit at least two of mentee's drafts of parent communication. Include strengths as well as tips for refinement.

Build Reflective Practice
- Write a summary of feedback. Attach copies of communication.

TIPS FOR DOCUMENTATION

Share with a mentee record keeping strategies you use for communication with parents and/or the ways you document student behaviors.

Build Reflective Practice
- Attach a blank form or example of the log you share with a brief summary of the interaction.

TEACHING SELF-ASSESSMENT

Use a copy of your district's evaluation form for assessing your teaching practice. Fill this out on yourself and share your personal reflections with your mentee.

Build Reflective Practice
- Write a summary of insights gained through your self-assessment and the professional sharing.

*Suggested follow-up: Ask mentee if he/she would like to assess him/herself with the evaluation instrument and conference with you regarding reflections. Provide specific mentoring assistance based on areas of need.

Second Thoughts: Journal Reflection

"If we wonder at the uniqueness of a snowflake, how much more must we stand in awe of the infinite variety we find in human beings?"

—JOSEPH AND LOIS BIRD

CHAPTER 3

Developing Teaching Skills and Support through Mentoring

> "Those who bring sunshine to the lives of others cannot keep it from themselves."
>
> —James Barrie

Many teachers never have the opportunity to observe a colleague. What a rich resource right next door! Opening our classroom to others creates an environment for dialogue, problem solving and affirming our own professional practices. To facilitate this growth activity, be creative. Cover another teacher's class during your prep time to allow that teacher to observe another. As a teacher leader, design a visitation schedule to provide teachers this enriching opportunity. Establishing a reciprocal visitation routine between you and your mentee will deepen your mentoring relationship. It will provide specificity to the conferencing, questioning and willingness to initiate strategies for continuous improvement. It also builds affirmation of mentee's strengths.

Visitation provides a broadening perspective for your mentee and a refreshing look at another teacher in action. By the mentor initiating the visitation process, the threat of having someone "watch you teach" is diminished. Once the comfort level of being in each other's classrooms is established, the growth can accelerate. The observation tools included in this chapter will provide methods to collect data for reflection. The tools are not meant to be evaluative; they produce feedback for self-assessment and goal setting.

The sharing and implementing of effective practices throughout a school results in systemic support. A campus that constructs this support structure will be a learning community for staff and students.

Your commitment to mentoring is important. The more specific you develop skills and learn information, coupled with your dedication, the greater the benefit to our profession.

> *"My positive investment to mentoring is to improve my leadership skills and indirectly work to improve the student's learning in my school by helping others (and myself) realize potential."*
>
> —Mentor's Commitment

Tip from Mentor Teacher

"Drop in mentee's classroom at the end of the day with an agenda for encouragement. The result can be a fresh start for the next day."

- ❏ Review discipline issues
- ❏ Confirm next meeting time
- ❏ Showcase mentee's progress
- ❏ Team an activity
- ❏ Update sub file
- ❏ Report cards
- ❏ Prepare for break
- ❏ Celebrate being a mentor!

Month _____

Sunday	Monday	Tuesday	Wednesday	Thursday	Friday	Saturday

Topics to Discuss with Mentee

- ❏ Professional roles and responsibilities
- ❏ Reflection of growth
- ❏ Instructional strategies

COPYRIGHT © KENDALL/HUNT PUBLISHING COMPANY

Professional Development Lesson Plan

TIP: *Give positive feedback, limit refinement comment to one.*

Subject: *Developing Teaching Skills and Support through Mentoring* Class/Period: *Seminar 3* Date: _____

Objectives

- Reflect on and celebrate personalized applications of effective mentoring.
- Learn observation techniques.
- Generate types of feedback with specific examples for mentee growth.
- Create a local brochure for increasing systemic support.

Teaching Standard: *Engages in Professional Development*

Set *Read introduction to chapter.*

Procedures

1. Think about knowledge and skills you have acquired. Write a Celebration (PR11) in relationship to your application of the knowledge or skills.

2. Read Classroom Data Collection Techniques (PR12). These tools are not intended to be used as evaluation tools. They have been included to provide you with data collection tools and/or a self-analysis tool to assist mentees in identifying areas for refinement. If you have an opportunity to observe your mentee, pre-conference to decide data that would be helpful to your mentee. Reciprocate by having your mentee observe you and collect data. Or, videotape a lesson and analyze together data collected.

3. Specific feedback will assist in your mentee's ability to continue to reinforce areas of teaching performed well and set goals in areas needing growth. By focusing on collected data, the teamwork is non-judgmental and supportive. Read the example on Sample Feedback: Reinforcement + Refinement (PR13). Think back to your last class taught and write a Celebration and Tip for Success for yourself as practice.

   Written feedback is beneficial because it can be referred to at a later time when needed.

4. Duplicate Feedback: Reinforcement + Refinement (PR14) for use in your mentoring relationship.

5. Read Systemic Support for Teacher Induction and Mentoring (PR15). Decide what you can do to promote teacher induction and mentoring at your site or in your district. Write a goal.

Procedures (continued)

6. Review *Sample Who, What, Where, When and How?: Mentor Brochure* (PRI6) for mentor topics to assist mentees. Personalize the information to your school or district. Use it to frame your work with your mentee. Create a finished brochure for your school or district and further systemic support in your educational system.

7. Lastly, reflect on your mentoring experience to date or your dedication to the process of mentoring and write a *Mentoring Commitment Letter* (PRI7) for future reference.

Closure/Self-Assessment/Reflection	Celebration!
❏ Content Related Reflection ❏ Second Thoughts: Journal Reflection	❏ Celebration (PRI1)

Extended Activities

❏ Mentor/Mentee Summary of Interaction
❏ Interactions Contact Log
❏ Choice Activities for Ongoing Professional Development

Note:
Practice →
↓
Reflect
↓
Document
↓
Apply →

Resources

❏ Calendar
❏ Tip
❏ Tip from Mentor Teacher
❏ Topics to Discuss with Mentee

Notes:

BEST
Beginning Educator Support Team

Celebration

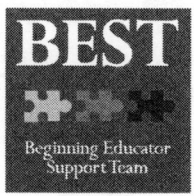

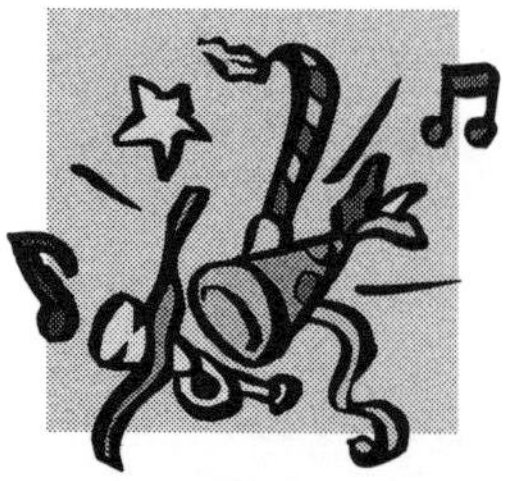

PR11

Classroom Data Collection Techniques

Teacher Verbalization

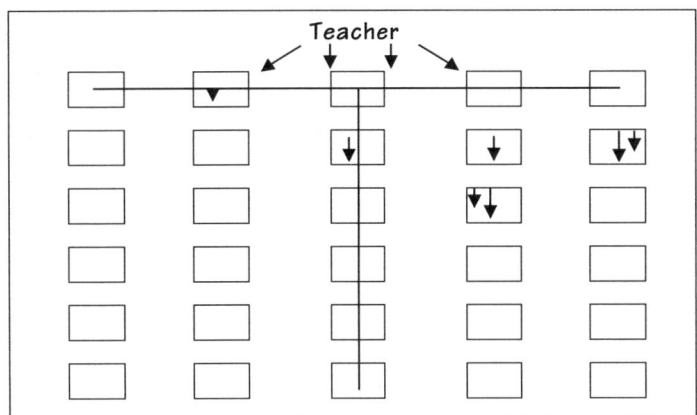

1. When the teacher asks a question of the whole class indicate with an arrow from the teacher box.

2. Draw an arrow in the student box when the teacher asks a specific student a question or when a student contributes.

T-Zone

Research shows that a predominant pattern of interaction exists in many classrooms. Typically, students in the front and center areas were called on more frequently.

Scripting

To further analyze teacher or student interactions script exact questions and/or responses. For example, to analyze a teacher's questioning techniques, record every question a teacher asks during a lesson or class period.

Teacher Movement

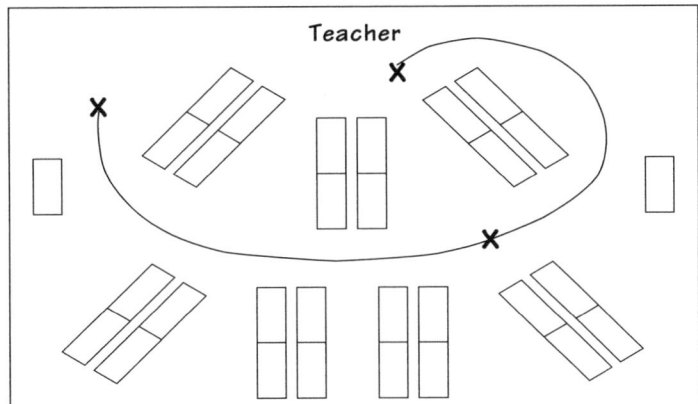

Mark with an X where the teacher begins the lesson or period. Draw a line representing teacher movement throughout the observation. Record times at regular intervals or at teacher pauses or stops in movement.

Classroom Data Collection Techniques

Student Verbalization

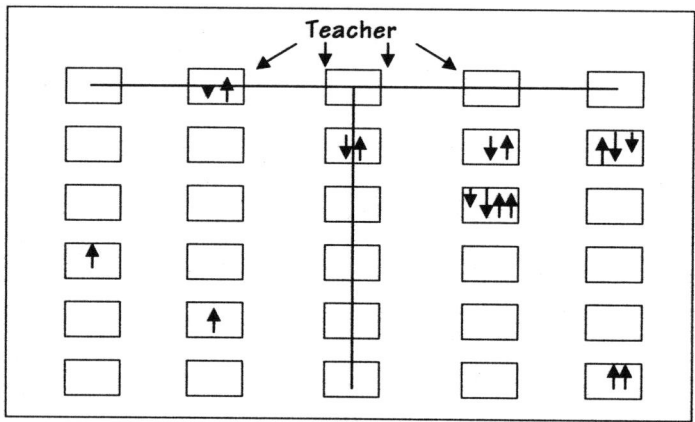

↑ In addition to charting teacher verbalization to individual students, draw arrows upward from individual student desks indicating student contributions or responses.

Student Behaviors

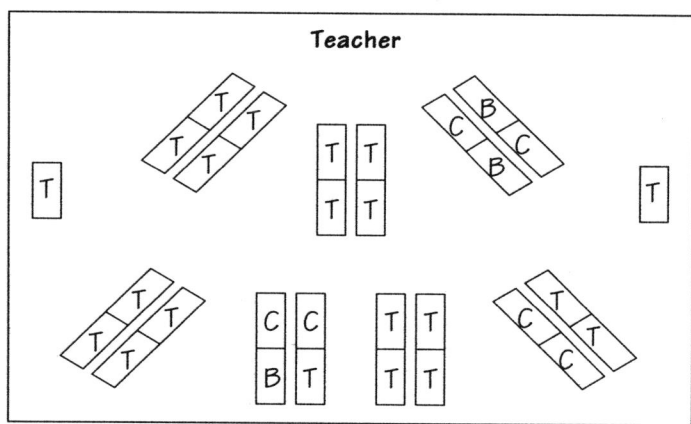

Create symbols to record student behaviors at various timed intervals.

LEGEND Example:

☐ On task = **T**

☐ Blurting = **B**

☐ Side conversations = **C**

PR12
Page 2 of 3

COPYRIGHT © KENDALL/HUNT PUBLISHING COMPANY

Classroom Data Collection Techniques

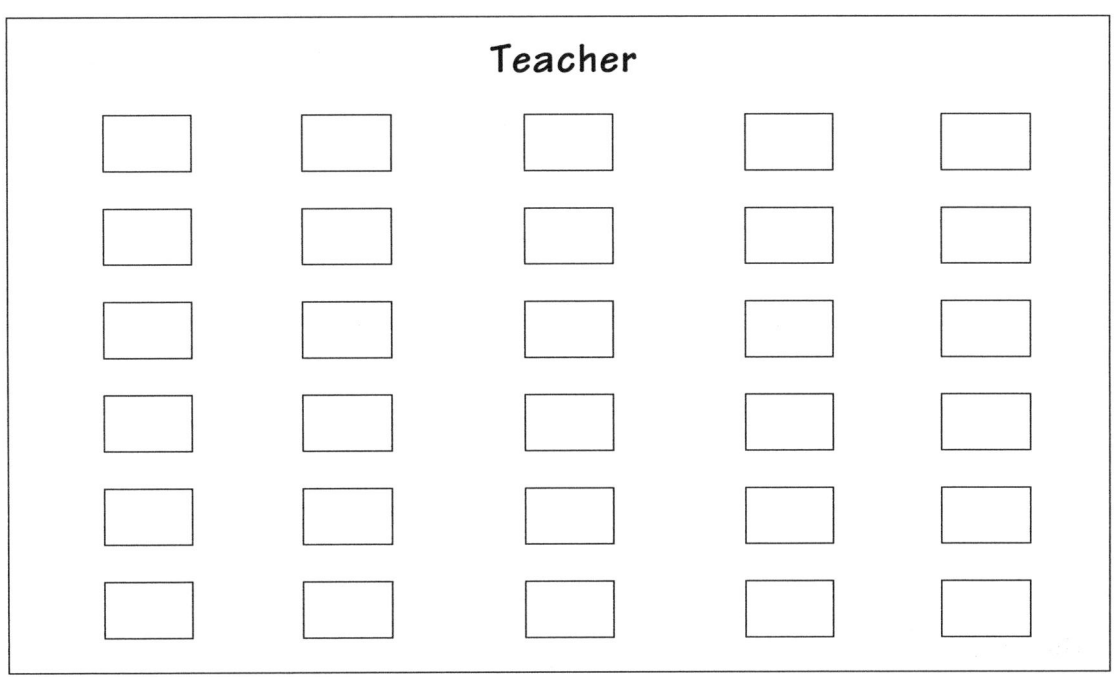

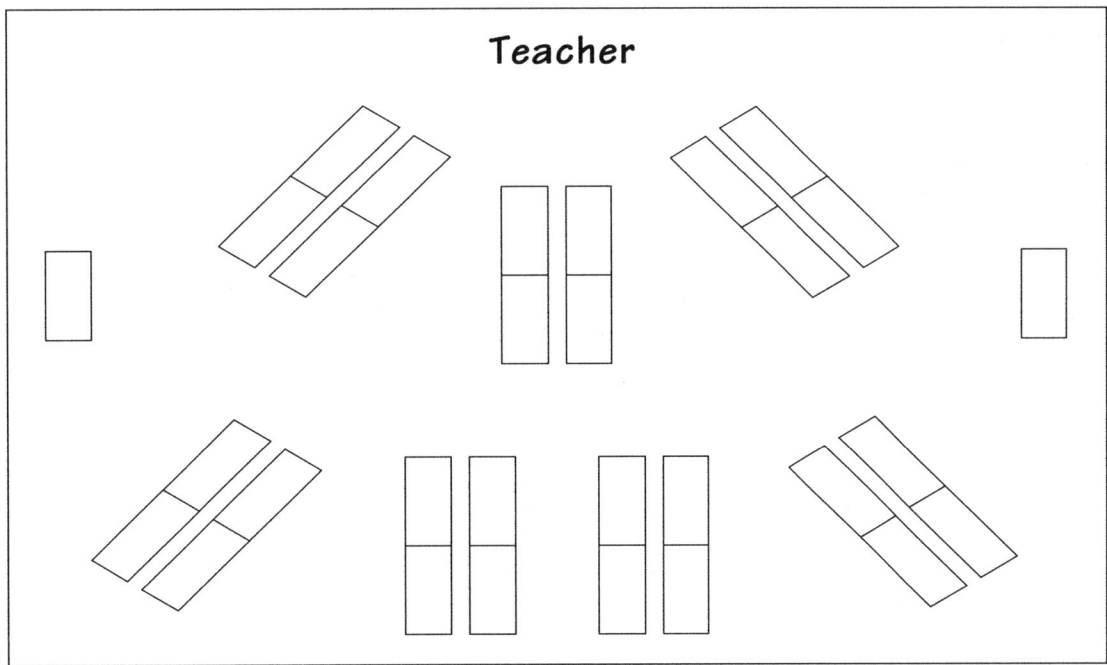

SAMPLE

Feedback: Reinforcement + Refinement

Celebration . . .
(Reinforcement)

You are seeking help from your grade level leader and reviewing orientation resource materials to assist in your area of challenge. This shows your persistence to analyze and resolve this issue. Celebrate the 99% of your classroom students that are meeting your expectations.

Tip for Success . . .
(Refinement)

Hold a private conference with disruptive student to discuss the issues and get to know the student better, which may be key to genuinely unlocking a solution. Be sure to highlight a strength of the student. A contract may be appropriate at the end of the conference to secure agreements made.

Feedback: Reinforcement + Refinement

Mentee _____ Mentor _____

Grade/Content _____ Date/Time _____

Celebration . . .
(Reinforcement)

Tip for Success . . .
(Refinement)

PR13

Feedback: Reinforcement + Refinement

Mentee _____ Mentor _____

Grade/Content _____ Date/Time _____

Celebration . . . (Reinforcement)	**Tip for Success . . .** (Refinement)

Feedback: Reinforcement + Refinement

Mentee _____ Mentor _____

Grade/Content _____ Date/Time _____

Celebration . . . (Reinforcement)	**Tip for Success . . .** (Refinement)

PR14

Systemic Support for Teacher Induction and Mentoring

Systemic support can be provided at the school site.

Veteran Teachers Can ...

- Offer new faculty curriculum, management plans, supplies, materials, furniture ...
- Welcome new faculty to campus so they will feel included and a part of a new professional team of educators; provide campus tour, accompany to staff meeting, introduce to key people, provide resources ...
- Include mentees in department or grade level meetings; ask for their input, facilitate their questions, ask for contributions ...
- Promote adjusted duty/responsibilities until new staff is adjusted ...
- Volunteer to be a "guide-on-the-side" ...
- Volunteer to be a mentor ...
- Record questions from new faculty. Provide any patterns to building administration for review and adjustments to support ...
- Other:

Building Administrators Can ...

- Consider one or no duties for new faculty ...
- Consider only one to two preps for middle or secondary level ...
- Provide curriculum materials and supplies in the classroom ...
- Observe classroom frequently to determine and respond to needs ...
- Be available for questions, concerns and challenges ...
- Avoid formal evaluation between October and November ...
- Select positive, professional role models to serve as mentors ...
- Articulate to mentors their role and responsibilities ...
- Encourage new faculty and mentors in ongoing professional growth ...
- Show appreciation for mentors' extra time and dedication to the profession ...
- Other:

Systemic support can also be provided district-wide.

District Administrators and/or Building Administrators Can . . .

- Limit committee participation to one per new staff . . .
- Provide a lower class size for first year . . .
- Avoid using a new teacher's classroom for summer school or other extracurricular activities . . .
- Limit the number of orientation days prior to beginning of school . . .
- Prior to the start of school, allow time for teachers to work in their classrooms . . .
- Schedule a series of seminars and training throughout the school year to capitalize on the developmental phases of new faculty . . .
- Expand teacher induction model to three years . . .
- Communicate district calendar, commitments and expectations . . .
- Promote teacher induction and mentoring through professional growth opportunities with incentives . . .
- Other:

What Can I Do to Make a Difference?

GOAL to further my school or district **SYSTEMIC SUPPORT**:

Sample

Who, What, Where, When and How?: Mentor Brochure

Create your own school or district *Who, What, Where, When and How?: Mentor Brochure* to assist mentors in facilitating their support of new faculty. Design your personalized brochure using the following generic content and format as a guide. Individualize each section with content that relates to your school site or district.

Vision/Mission: What Are We About?

Key People to Know: Who?

- Principal
- Secretary
- Custodial Staff
- School Nurse
- Attendance Clerk
- Mentor
- Grade Level Peers
- District Office Support
- Resource Staff
- Registrar
- Psychologist
- Other
-

- Speech Pathologist
- Counselor
- Librarian
- Aides
- Cafeteria Staff
- Security
- Therapist
- Productions/AV Clerk
- Computer Support Person
- Personnel Director
- Curriculum Specialist
- Other
-

Auxiliary Tools: Where and How to Use?

- Phone system
- Substitute System (Phone#-Preferred sub)
- Copy Machine
- Laminating Machine
- Die Cut Machine
- Button/Badge Machine
- Mail System
- Other
-

- TV/VCR
- Intercom System/Announcements
- Computer Labs/Technology
- Soda, Candy Machine, Microwave
- Facilities
- Student Bookstore
- Internet
- Other
-

Materials: How to Obtain?

- Warehouse Orders
- Purchase Orders
- Library Books
- Literature Library
- Bubble Sheets
- Other
-

- Gradebooks (Gradebook +)
- Video Resources
- Transportation
- Gold Files
- Math, Science, Social Studies, Art Resources
- Other
-

Standards and Curriculum: What Are the Expectations?

- State Standards
- Indicators of Learning
- Curriculum Framework
- CRE Objectives
- Other
-

- TDR (Elementary)
- Vocational Competencies
- NCA Goals
- Student Learning Goal
- Other
-

Calendar Events: What's Happening, When?

- Conference Week
- In-service Days
- Winter Break, Spring Break
- Early Release Days
- Site Events (Carnivals, Festivals)
- Faculty Meetings
- District Calendar
- Other
-

- Curriculum Night—Open House
- Daily Announcements
- Graduation
- Promotion
- Plays, Music Productions, Concerts
- Bookstore Days
- Testing Dates
- Other
-

Assessment Instruments: What and When?

- AIMS
- Running Records
- SAT 9
- CRE's
- Other
-

- ABACUS
- Non-Competitive Testing/Grades
- Special Education Testing
- Other Assessments
- Other
-

Procedures: What and How?

- Attendance
- Lunch Cards
- Discipline
- Attire (Students, Staff)
- Volunteers
- Emergencies
- Fire Drills
- Evacuations
- Lesson Plans
- Sign-Out
- 504/IEP/IVEP Plans
- Committees
- Curriculum
- Other

- Field Trips
- Crisis Plan/Suicidal Plan
- PRIDE
- Assemblies
- Health Office
- Early Release Schedule
- Recess (Elementary)
- Duties
- Bomb Threat
- Re-certification
- Chaperone Responsibilities
- Facilities Usage
- Other

Forms: Where to Locate and How to Process?

- Progress Reports
- Report Cards
- Field Trip
- Permission Slips
- Personnel Action Request
- Attendance Referrals/Bubble
- Announcement Form
- Requisitions
- Equipment Check-out
- Special Ed Referrals
- Other

- Hall, Nurse, Office Passes
- Video/Film Check-out
- Child Study Referrals
- Maps
- Referral Forms
- Citations
- Student Study Team
- Work Orders
- Activity Requests
- Other

Special Area Support: Who?

- Resource
- Hearing Impaired
- Occupational Therapist
- Teaching Assistants
- Core Techs
- Career Center
- Music/PE
- Other

- Speech Therapist
- Physical Therapist
- Reading Specialist
- Subject Liaisons
- Vocational Director
- Long-term Sub
- Other

Mentoring Commitment Letter

Date _____

(Stem Choice)

❑ As a result of today learning I will participate in my mentoring partnership by . . .

❑ I now realize that to have an effective learning experience as a mentor, I will . . .

❑ I bring the following strengths and will contribute them to the mentoring partnership by . . .

❑ My hopes or positive expectations for my mentoring partnership include _____
and my first step in meeting these objectives is to _____

_____
(Signature)

Content Related Reflection

Respond to one of the following questions:

- ❑ How are you fostering your mentoring relationship?
- ❑ How are you offering support or assistance to your mentee?
- ❑ What reflective questioning stems are you practicing?
- ❑ How are you individualizing your support based on your mentee's personality?

Mentor/Mentee Summary of Interaction*

Mentor Teacher Information
Name _____
District _____
School _____
Grade Level/Content Area _____

Mentee Teacher Information
Name _____
District _____
School _____
Grade Level/Content Area _____

Contact Information
Date of Contact _____
   Beginning Time _____
   Ending Time _____
   Total Time _____

Contact Initiated By
❏ Mentor Teacher   ❏ Mentee Teacher

Type of Contact
❏ One-on-One   ❏ Drop-in Visit
❏ Journal   ❏ Classroom Observation
❏ Phone Call   ❏ Conference
❏ E-mail   ❏ Other _____

Questions/Issues to Address with Mentee:

Ideas Generated During Interaction:

Practical Applications:

*This form is to be duplicated as many times as needed. Create a section in your portfolio to file all interaction documentation.

COPYRIGHT © KENDALL/HUNT PUBLISHING COMPANY   Permission to duplicate for personal, non-commercial use.

Interactions Contact Log*

Date	Meeting Time	Total Time	Contact Initiated By Mentor Teacher or Mentee Teacher	Type of Contact One-on-One/Phone Call/ E-mail/Journal/Drop-in Visit/ Classroom Observation/ Conference/Other

*This form is to be duplicated as many times as needed. Create a section in your portfolio to file all interaction documentation.

Choice Activities for Ongoing Professional Development

TEACHER SEMINAR

Attend a scheduled BEST seminar designed for new teachers or another seminar with your mentee. Record notes and questions. Discuss content and application with mentee.

Build Reflective Practice

- Write a summary of your insights and discussion.

STUDENT BEHAVIORS: PREVENTION/INTERVENTION

Generate a list of typical inappropriate student behaviors for the age level of students you teach. Next to each behavior, write a tip for how to prevent this behavior. Next, generate a teacher response that might guide the misbehavior back to appropriate behavior. Utilize the list as you interact on discipline/management issues with your mentee. Reminder: Affirm positive delivery.

Build Reflective Practice

- File your list with student behaviors, recommended teacher responses and intervention strategies for a resource.

- Attach a summary of the benefits to your mentoring.

MODELING PROFESSIONALISM FOR NEW TEACHERS

Invite your mentee to attend a committee or leadership-oriented meeting with you. Debrief by reviewing professional skills that you consciously used during the meeting.

Build Reflective Practice

- Write a summary of insights this activity provided for you and the importance of modeling professionalism to new colleagues.

Second Thoughts: Journal Reflection

"With desire and commitment the leader builds a fire inside that causes others to glow brightly. No matter what the odds, the leader knows that any task can be accomplished."

—HARRY K. AND ROSEMARY T. WONG

CHAPTER 4

Analyzing and Planning for Professional Growth through Mentoring

> "We cannot direct the wind . . . but we can adjust the sails."
>
> —Anonymous

As the year progresses, your mentoring focus will change based on developing mentee's needs, adjustment to school community, instructional skills, content knowledge and confidence. Your goal in the mentoring process is to have your mentee become a reflective practitioner. Through practicing, reflecting, documenting and applying new learning, your mentee will create a process for self-improvement in ongoing professional growth.

You have probably already sensed the change in your role as a mentor. You have moved through a cycle that initiated with many questions and logistics and has progressed to more specific concerns. Your mentoring must continue to be deliberate. The next cycle is to identify with the mentee areas of reinforcement and refinement. Many times at this stage of mentoring, a mentee does not know the questions to ask to meet needs or thinks mentoring is no longer needed because the questions of immediacy have been answered. Mentoring is viewed as taking care of the logistics and helping with the emotional adjustment to the position but not directly connected to teaching practice. This is in part because it was how mentoring was initially defined by mentee's needs and by you as a mentor responding to the developmental phase of your mentee.

By utilizing your mentoring skills you can continue to promote mentee growth. This is the time to become intentional about making a natural transition to mentee's self-reflection and identifying areas for growth. It is your leadership in the mentoring partnership that will enable a mutual advance to the next phase of your relationship. The change process will be gradual but you can apply specific mentoring techniques to grow the best. This is the time when your mentee is past the immediacy of surviving day to day and has the emotional and professional capacity to question practice and build patterns in teaching that will effect students for years to come. Help your mentee define best teaching practice and develop skills aligned to teaching expectations. Capture these moments to build effective teaching capacity.

In the mentoring cycle, you will revert from a more collaborative approach back to direct due to a specific area of need, but will rebound to more and more autonomy, decision making and collaboration from the mentee in areas of classroom instruction, management, subject matter, assessment and working with parents and others. Mentees, like students, all have differentiated needs. Assess your mentee's progress. Monitor and adjust. Set new goals to make the most of your mentoring.

If your mentoring interactions have lessened, analyze the reasons why. Become intentional about re-instating the vigorous routine established previously. The purpose is more important than ever. Your care in the relationship to this point has provided an avenue to build growth—capitalize now.

Tip from Mentor Teacher

"Just knowing you are there makes a world of difference."

✓ POINTS

- ❏ Revisit professional goal
- ❏ Establish journaling practice
- ❏ Practice reflective questioning
- ❏ Attend professional conference with mentee
- ❏ Classroom dynamics
- ❏ Warm-up exercises
- ❏ Guest speaker
- ❏ Student self-assessments

Month _____

Sunday	Monday	Tuesday	Wednesday	Thursday	Friday	Saturday

Topics to Discuss with Mentee

- ❏ Redefine expectations of mentor/mentee relationship
- ❏ Assess new classroom strategy implemented
- ❏ Discuss differentiation strategies

Professional Development Lesson Plan

TIP: *Be on time. Be honest. Listen. Be flexible.*
Model professionalism.

Subject *Analyzing and Planning for Professional Growth through Mentoring*   Class/Period *Seminar 4*   Date _____

Objectives

- Review acquired mentoring skills and reflect on mentoring experience.
- Describe, analyze and assess from mentoring partnership characteristic essential to ongoing professional development.
- Read and diagnose competency in mentoring elements that facilitate growth in a mentee.
- Learn stages of mentoring cycle to assess mentoring relationship and set goals.

Teaching Standard *Engages in Professional Development*

Set
Read introduction to chapter.

Procedures

1. Reflect on your mentoring in the areas of interpersonal and technical skills, reflective practice and procedural knowledge that are positively impacting your mentoring relationship.

2. Complete the *Mentoring Acrostic* (PR18) based on your definition of and experience with a mentoring partnership. Use words, phrases or sentences. Review with a mentor colleague or with your mentee as a communication tool.

3. Review from PR19 the *Ten Characteristics of Effective Mentoring Relationships*. Analyze, assess and record an example and evidence of applied practice from your own mentoring experience. Star (★) an area where you are exemplar and check (✓) an area for further refinement.

4. Read *How the Mentoring Relationship Facilitates Protégé Growth* (PR20). After reading, star (★) an element where you demonstrate competency and check (✓) an element for professional growth.

Procedures (continued)

5. Review the graphic of *The Mentoring Cycle* (PR21). Read the definition of the three mentoring approaches in the "Notes" section of this lesson plan. Transfer knowledge to "Definitions of Mentoring Approaches" on PR21 by rephrasing based on your understanding or by creating a graphic to represent the approach. In "Behaviors of Mentees and Mentors" list mentee and mentor behaviors for each approach based on your knowledge of mentoring and your own experience. On the "Placement in the Mentoring Cycle," identify where you are with your mentee. Think about the flexibility of the cycle based on the areas of strength or need of your mentee. Based on the situation, you could be in all three areas within a given conference time. Based on your assessment, create a goal in "Goal for Continued Progress in the Mentoring Cycle."

6. Celebrate your influence on the teaching profession by your commitment to mentoring. Become deliberate about increasing skills and competencies based on mentees areas of need. Reflecting on your practice, align your mentoring to placement in the mentoring cycle to impact the growth of your mentee at a faster rate.

Closure/Self-Assessment/Reflection	Celebration!
☐ *Content Related Reflection* ☐ *Second Thoughts: Journal Reflection*	☐

Extended Activities

☐ *Mentor/Mentee Summary of Interaction*
☐ *Interactions Contact Log*
☐ *Choice Activities for Ongoing Professional Development*

Note:
Practice ←
↓
Reflect
↓
Document
↓
Apply ⎯⎯

Resources

☐ *Calendars** ☐ *Tip from Mentor*
☐ *Tip* ☐ *Topics to Discuss with Mentee*

*An additional calendar is added in this chapter to allow calendaring for additional months at the end of the school year.

Notes:

The Mentoring Cycle

Direct

In the <u>Direct</u> approach, the mentor takes the lead in the relationship, initiating interactions and offering support and solutions. Routine tasks and information are provided.

Assist

In the <u>Assist</u> approach, the mentor continues to initiate contact the majority of the time, uses skills to invite the mentee to begin to reflect on his/her own practice and offers possible solutions to challenges.

Collaborate

In the <u>Collaborate</u> approach, the mentor and mentee share equally in initiating interactions, analyzing and reflecting on their practice and facilitating mutual professional development.

Celebration: Mentoring Acrostic

PR18

Ten Characteristics of Effective Mentoring Relationships*

Characteristics	Evidence of Applied Practice
1. Mutual and reciprocal	
2. Trusting	
3. Confidential	
4. Purposeful and productive	
5. Positive and respectful	
6. Supportive and encouraging	
7. Collaborative	
8. Developmental and evolving over time	
9. Reflective and growth-oriented	
10. Based on accurate communication	

*Characteristics from *Mentoring to Improve Schools*, ASCD, 1999.

PR19

How the Mentoring Relationship Facilitates Protégé Growth

What is it that will help create the conditions for new teachers to learn all that is expected of professionals and to find success as reflective, student-centered educators—without becoming overwhelmed by this daunting process, to the point of leaving the profession or focusing exclusively on their own survival? About 20 years of research and experience has shown that the answer to this dilemma is an effective mentor-protégé relationship. Although many experienced educators did not have the benefit of such a supportive relationship, they know how isolated they felt as beginners and how slow and awkward trial and error learning was. They also recognize that collaborative support from trusted colleagues is the best context for learning to be an effective teacher.

There is no substitute for experience—yet gaining sufficient insight and wisdom through trial and error experiences is not an effective way to learn, nor is it responsive to students' immediate need for an effective teacher. Learning is the result of doing something one has not done before and discovering through that experience how to do it successfully. By working with and learning from the experience of a mentor, the process can be greatly accelerated, the stress greatly reduced, and success as a teacher achieved more frequently.

Typically novice teachers expect that their learning process will be challenging, and they are generally quite open to learning from others, as long as the assistance is supportive, positive, and productive. On the other hand, novice teachers also know that they must quickly demonstrate their ability as a teacher and feel they should not make too many mistakes for fear they will appear incompetent. These two issues place novice teachers in a dilemma.

- Without the context and support for professional learning, novice teachers often become veteran teachers who stick to their "tried and true" teaching methods and resist professional changes that are necessary evolutions in effective practice.

- With a supportive context for professional learning, novice teachers find success and self-confidence. They become veteran teachers who continually seek better ways to support student learning and who know from their own experience how to provide the needed context for learning for their own students.

How Mentors Facilitate the Process of Learning

To help beginning teachers develop professionally, five elements must be present.

1. The learner's personal needs must be met so there are no obstacles to learning and there is energy to deal with a change. For example, a new employee who hasn't yet found housing will probably have difficulty giving sufficient time to preparation for the next day's teaching. This does not suggest that a mentor's responsibilities include helping the protégé find housing, but an administrator might address that need by providing apartment listings and contact information or a bulletin board. However, it is the mentor's job to help the protégé with other needs such as classroom organization and the location of instructional resources.

2. Learners must have a personal goal to work toward that is defined relative to an effective, research-based model, such as a district's model of effective teaching and learning or a set of teaching standards. However, the goal for improvement must be chosen by the learner, although she may do so as a result of feedback from a principal's evaluation conference or a coaching conference with the mentor.

3. Support, assistance, excellent modeling, and encouragement must be available. Students' education demands that educators provide faster, more successful ways of helping one other develop professionally. For example, it is possible for new teachers to discover over time and on their own that effective instructional activities are a necessary element of classroom discipline. However, seeing that strategy demonstrated by a mentor and working with the mentor to practice and master using it as a much more powerful and certainly a faster method of learning it.

4. Educators must have a low-risk environment in which mistakes are seen as a part of the process of learning and becoming effective teachers. One of the major reasons that a confidential mentoring relationship is used is because teacher evaluation sometimes prompts a "dog and pony show" response rather than an open discussion of problems and areas for growth. This does not occur because school principals lack the skills to prompt true growth but rather because of the high-risk context of teacher evaluation. This is why mentors are often separated from evaluative roles.

From *Mentoring to Improve Schools, Facilitator's Guide* by ASCD. Alexandria, Va.: Association for Supervision and Curriculum Development, Copyright © 1999 ASCD. Reprinted by permission. All rights reserved.

When new teachers feel they must be seen as competent, they will resort to tried and true methods that closely control the learning environment but that may limit students' active involvement and learning. A quiet classroom is a good one, right? When new teachers know their mentor has confidence in them and their ability to learn—and when the mentors themselves have modeled learning from mistakes and a desire to grow—then the focus is on improvement, not just minimal competence.

5. An appropriate level of difficulty is provided in each new teaching task so that it is challenging enough to prompt the protégé's growth yet manageable enough to make the protégé's persistence and success likely. Growth requires learning how to successfully do new things. The mentor's assistance and experience should provide the delicate balance of sufficient challenge and support, but striking that balance requires an excellent knowledge of the protégé's strengths and needs. Therefore, mentors need training, practice, and support in assessing protégé needs and strengths. They also should prompt protégé reflection and a discussion of how to provide that balance in student learning in the teachers' own classroom.

Building an Effective Mentor-Protégé Relationship

The likelihood of creating an effective mentor-protégé relationship is increased by selecting mentors who already have many of the desired qualities. That is why carefully constructed and frequently refined mentor selection and matching processes and criteria are needed. Still, despite attempts to select mentors with these abilities, mentoring has its ups and downs and requires a long-term commitment.

Mentors and protégés must know how they need to act to work together successfully, they must be committed to trying to act that way more and more each day, and they must be mutually forgiving as they work together to practice and to learn how to act. This suggests that the training and support of mentors and their protégés in these skills and dispositions is crucial.

Mentors and protégés need to know the process for facilitating growth in others so that they may improve their ability to support each other's professional growth and ultimately use this process in their classrooms. In this way, mentoring is a model of excellent teaching and is a practice educators need to become better teachers.

END

The Mentoring Cycle

Definitions of Mentoring Approaches

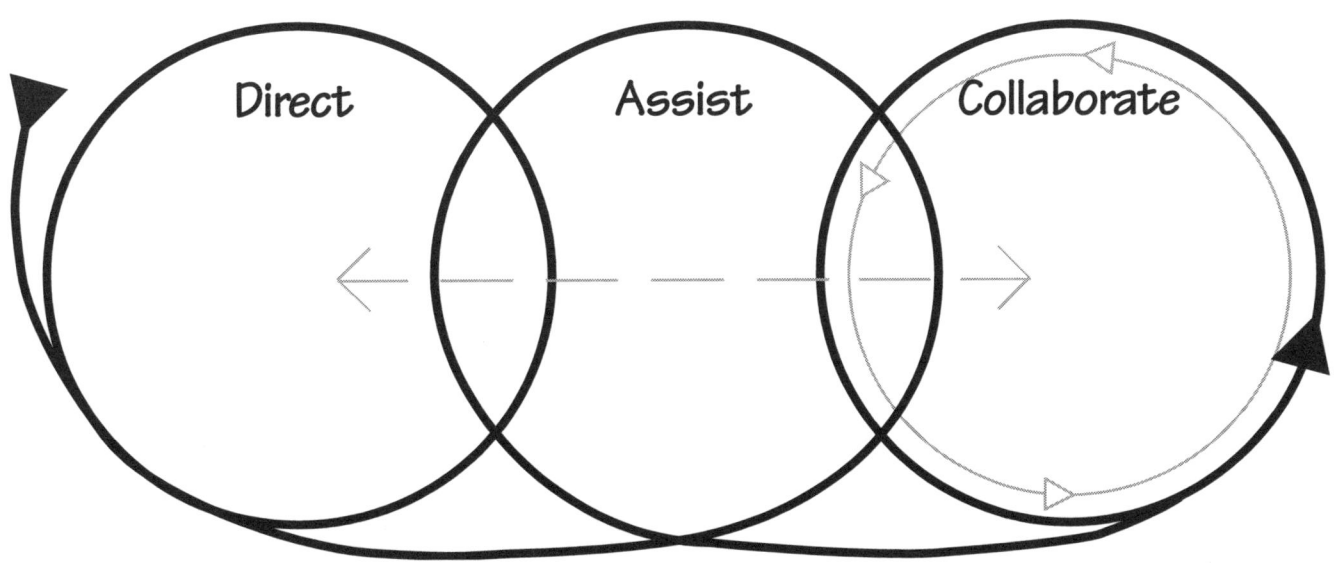

Behaviors of Mentees and Mentors

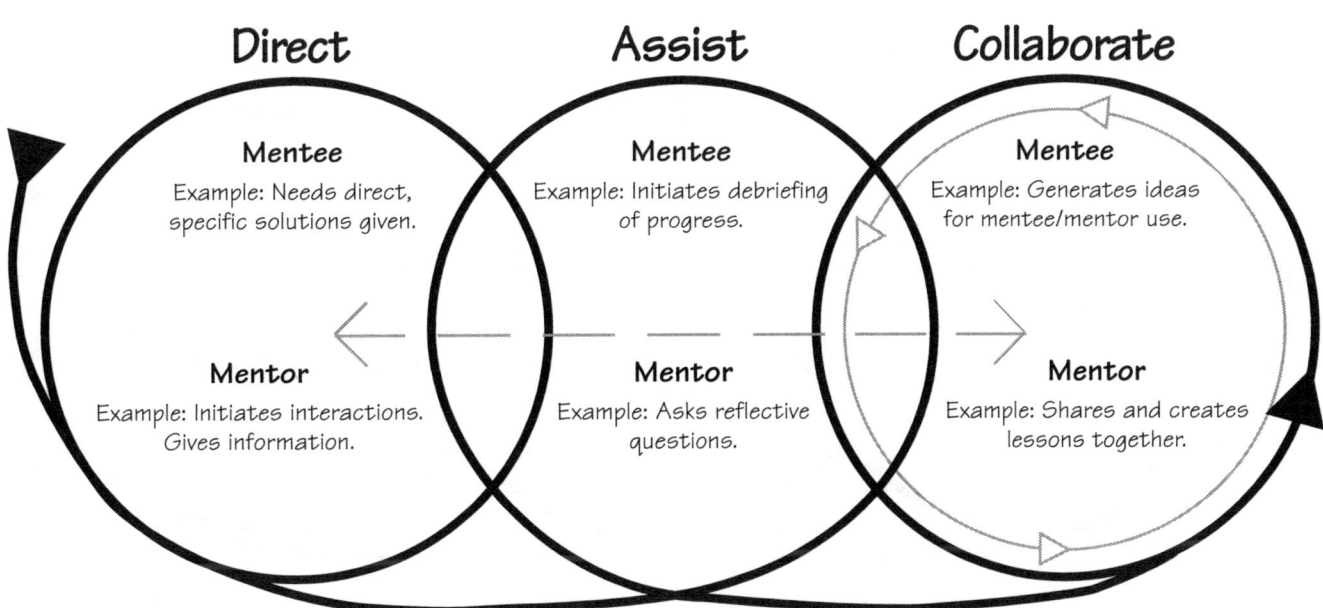

The Mentoring Cycle

(continued)

Placement in The Mentoring Cycle

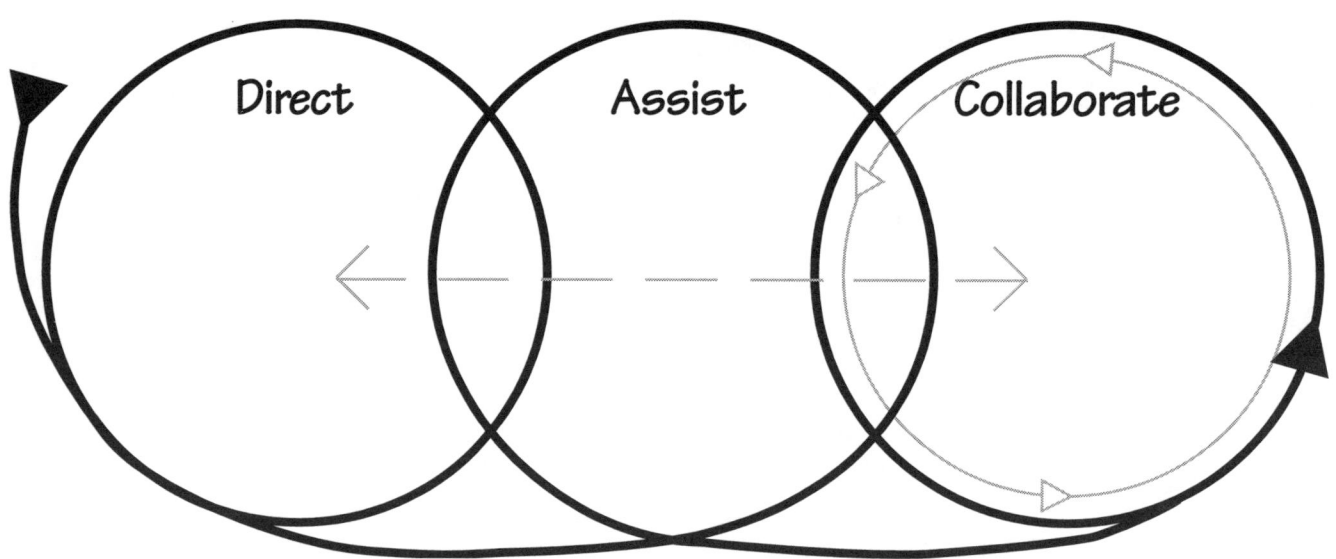

Goal for Continued Progress on the Mentoring Cycle

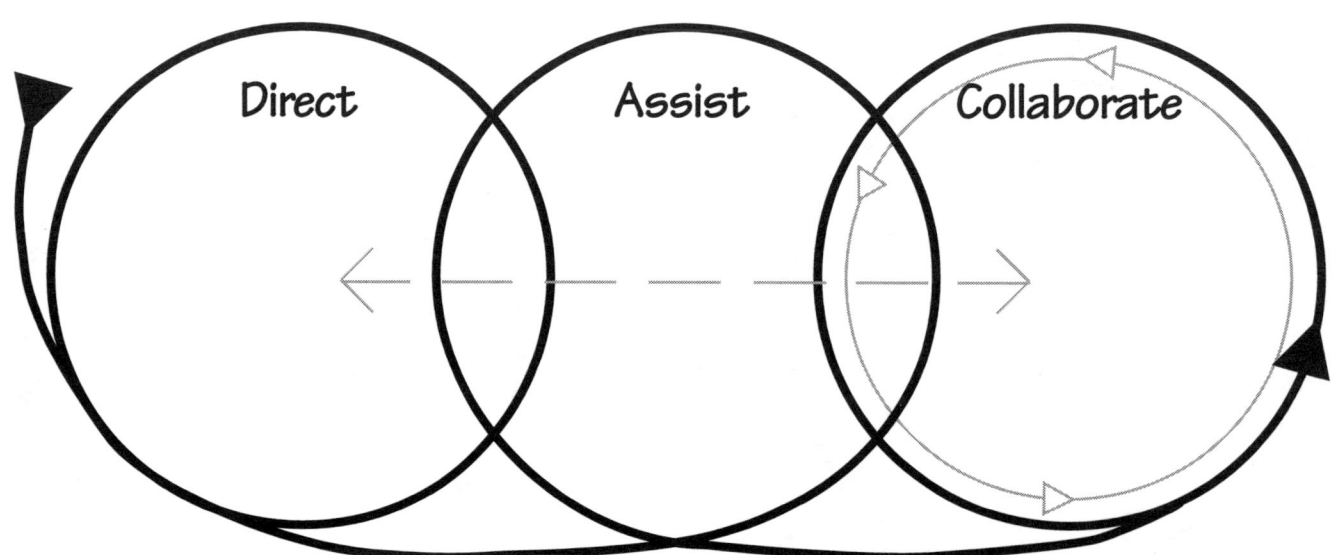

Content Related Reflection

Based on your self-identification checked (✓) for refinement on *Ten Characteristics of Effective Mentoring Relationships* (PR19), write a goal for applied practice.

Based on your self identification checked (✓) for professional growth on PR20 *How the Mentoring Relationship Facilitates Protégé Growth*, write a goal for immediate implementation.

Mentor/Mentee Summary of Interaction*

Mentor Teacher Information
Name _____
District _____
School _____
Grade Level/Content Area _____

Mentee Teacher Information
Name _____
District _____
School _____
Grade Level/Content Area _____

Contact Information
Date of Contact _____
  Beginning Time _____
  Ending Time _____
  Total Time _____
Contact Initiated By
❏ Mentor Teacher   ❏ Mentee Teacher

Type of Contact
❏ One-on-One   ❏ Drop-in Visit
❏ Journal   ❏ Classroom Observation
❏ Phone Call   ❏ Conference
❏ E-mail   ❏ Other _____

Questions/Issues to Address with Mentee:

Ideas Generated During Interaction:

Practical Applications:

*This form is to be duplicated as many times as needed. Create a section in your portfolio to file all interaction documentation.

Interactions Contact Log*

Date	Meeting Time	Total Time	Contact Initiated By Mentor Teacher or Mentee Teacher	Type of Contact One-on-One/Phone Call/ E-mail/Journal/Drop-in Visit/ Classroom Observation/ Conference/Other

*This form is to be duplicated as many times as needed. Create a section in your portfolio to file all interaction documentation.

Choice Activities for Ongoing Professional Development

TABLE TALK: PROFESSIONAL TOPIC

Select a professional topic of common interest to you and your mentee. Have a professional dialogue on the topic. Reminder: Walk away with a decision for follow-up or implementation.

Build Reflective Practice
- Summarize your dialogue.

SYSTEMIC VIEW POINT

Create a plan for orientating your mentee to the broader educational system, which could include district goals, board meeting, budgeting procedures, statewide mandates, educational organizations.

Build Reflective Practice
- Write a summary including your plan, implementation and key learnings as a mentor.

REFLECTIVE QUESTIONING REVIEW

Reflect on your ability to use questioning to foster mentee's individual self-analysis. Referring back to Chapter 2, monitor use of reflective questioning. Implement further as you move in the mentoring cycle.

Build Reflective Practice
- Summarize your assessment and plan for further development in this technical skill.

Tip from Mentor Teacher

"Give mentee choices in types of assistance within the mentoring relationship."

✓POINTS

- ❑ Acknowledge mentee's work
- ❑ Share a computer tip
- ❑ Analyze videotaped lesson
- ❑ Trade classes for a lesson
- ❑ Applied research
- ❑ Progress reports
- ❑ Faculty meeting contribution
- ❑ Budget time: Document material needs for next year

Month _____

Sunday	Monday	Tuesday	Wednesday	Thursday	Friday	Saturday

Topics to Discuss with Mentee

- ❑ Request specific data collection in my classroom
- ❑ Re-assess equity of learning for all students
- ❑ Review portfolio documents

COPYRIGHT © KENDALL/HUNT PUBLISHING COMPANY

Second Thoughts: Journal Reflection

"Education is growth . . . Education is not a preparation for life; education is life itself."
—JOHN DEWEY

CHAPTER 5

Strengthening Teacher Practices through Mentoring

> "Unless you try to do something beyond what you have already mastered, you will never grow."
>
> —Ralph Waldo Emerson

As an experienced educator, your professional routine includes assessing your practice for continual refinement. As mentors, where do we start to mentor a peer in the process of self-assessment and reflection with all there is to learn about our profession? Of course, as you learned in the previous chapter, the relationship initiates with questions and logistics. It progresses with application in a variety of mentoring strategies. Teaching standards are the next step that provide an extension of the mentoring process that deepens the context of teaching through a framework for professional growth. The common areas of expectation are identified. Examples include:

- Designs and plans instruction
- Creates and maintains a learning climate and
- Implements and manages instruction.

Formats designed for growth can be personalized to meet your mentee's development. Your state may or may not have instituted teaching standards. But every educational institution has teacher expectations, an evaluation tool with competencies. Create a mentoring plan to assist your mentee in assessment and a continual process of refining teaching practice.

Through the process of your mentee aligning practice to benchmarks and continually raising the bar, student performance will be positively effected. A teacher who is mentored with this framework will be able to internalize the reasons for decision making in the classroom. Equipped to label professional growth and to share with others will perpetuate the ongoing progression of better and better teaching.

Incorporate the standards framework into conferencing with your mentee in specific performance areas. Try a new approach. Create a journal communication. Use it as a tool to ask specific questions for reflection. Choose areas based on observable needs and the schema of the standards. Use them as a map to mentoring. Practice mentoring by design.

Tip from Mentor Teacher

"Be deliberate in stretching your mentoring to capitalize on teacher development for the mentee and the students' benefit."

✓ POINTS

- ❑ Review teaching standards/expectations
- ❑ Implement a new technique
- ❑ Identify strengths
- ❑ Document growth with portfolio artifacts
- ❑ Teacher evaluation
- ❑ Classroom energizers
- ❑ Thank you's
- ❑ Parent survey

Month _____

Sunday	Monday	Tuesday	Wednesday	Thursday	Friday	Saturday

Topics to Discuss with Mentee

- ❑ Help mentee plan administrator visit
- ❑ Promotion/retention regulations
- ❑ Discuss future contribution opportunities to school community

Professional Development Lesson Plan

TIP: Use teaching standards for showcasing strengths and identifying areas for growth.

Subject _Strengthening Teacher Practices through Mentoring_   Class/Period _Seminar 5_   Date _____

Objectives

- Preview teaching standards.
- Create examples of BEST practice within each standard.
- Process ways to facilitate mentee's professional growth in relationship to the standards.
- Design and role-play conferences.

Teaching Standard _Engages in Professional Development_

Set _Read introduction to chapter._

Procedures

1. Read _Examples of Standards_ (PR23).

2. Collect copy of your teaching evaluation instrument and, if developed, your state's standards in teaching.

3. Record on _Examples of Standards_ any adjustments to reflect own state's standards or categories from evaluation tool.

4. In the boxes provided on _Examples of Standards_, write an application of each standard to the mentoring process. Use your knowledge of the teaching expectations to define the framework for growth to the teaching profession. Set aside for use in _Content Related Reflection_.

5. When mentoring is planned, inclusion of learned skills and information can be prepared and utilized for more in-depth assistance. Complete _Mentoring by Design_ (PR23) to experience the various considerations for response.

6. Another approach of communication in mentoring is through journaling. Sometimes one-on-one conferencing is not possible. A journal can facilitate those times. A journal can be used for your mentee to record questions/concerns. You can respond by writing your mentoring advice or reflective questions. Practice on _Journal Entry_ (PR24) responding to a current mentee issue or proposed question. Prior to writing your answer, read the _Journaling Considerations_ and _General Journaling Tips_. After writing, read and then note your own reaction to the exercise in the _Feedback Box_ for future reference.

Closure/Self-Assessment/Reflection	Celebration!
❏ *Content Related Reflection* ❏ *Second Thoughts: Journal Reflection*	❏

Extended Activities

❏ *Mentor/Mentee Summary of Interaction*
❏ *Interactions Contact Log*
❏ *Choice Activities for Ongoing Professional Development*

Note:
Practice ←
↓
Reflect
↓
Document
↓
Apply ⟶

Resources

❏ *Calendar* ❏ *Tip from Mentor Teacher*
❏ *Tip* ❏ *Topics to Discuss with Mentee*

Notes:

Examples of Standards

Standard 1: Designs and Plans Instruction	Standard 2: Creates and Maintains a Learning Climate	Standard 3: Implements and Manages Instruction
Standard 4: Assesses Learning and Communicates Results	Standard 5: Collaborates with Colleagues, Parents, and Others	Standard 6: Engages in Professional Development
Standard 7: Demonstrates Content Knowledge	Standard 8: Demonstrates Professional Knowledge	Standard 9: Implements Special Education Components

PR22

Mentoring by Design

Directions:
1. Choose a mentoring scenario from the choices below.
2. Create a conference plan to address the mentee issue in a one-on-one meeting.
   - Utilize teaching standards in conference plan.
   - Consider previously learned mentoring practices.
     - —Phases
     - —Behaviors of Effective Mentors
     - —Reflective Questioning
     - —Systemic Support
     - —Successful Partnerships
     - —Personality and Interaction Styles
     - —Specific Feedback
     - —Mentoring Continuum

Scenario Options. Check One.
- ❏ Mentee shares continuous frustration about students who are not on-task.
- ❏ Mentee is reluctant to work with mentor.

Conference Plan

Role-Play*

Notes for Future Conference Use

*Role-playing your conference plan will benefit future conferences.

PR23

Journal Entry

Current Mentee Issue/Question

Journaling Considerations
- ☐ Teaching Standards
- ☐ Mentoring Continuum
- ☐ Behaviors of Effective Mentors
  - Building Trust
  - Communicates Effectively
  - Cultivating Confidence
  - Developing Competence
- ☐ Systemic Support
- ☐ Specific Feedback
- ☐ Reflective Questions
- ☐ Personality/Interaction Styles

General Journaling Tips
- ☐ Include celebration
- ☐ Provide journaling format
- ☐ Establish journaling routine
- ☐ Collect as artifact for mentor and mentee portfolios

Mentor Journal Entry

Feedback Box

PR24

Content Related Reflection

What's Next?

How will you initiate and implement the teaching standards to facilitate professional growth in your mentee?

Mentor/Mentee Summary of Interaction*

Mentor Teacher Information
Name _____
District _____
School _____
Grade Level/Content Area _____

Mentee Teacher Information
Name _____
District _____
School _____
Grade Level/Content Area _____

Contact Information
Date of Contact _____
   Beginning Time _____
   Ending Time _____
   Total Time _____

Contact Initiated By
❑ Mentor Teacher ❑ Mentee Teacher

Type of Contact
❑ One-on-One ❑ Drop-in Visit
❑ Journal ❑ Classroom Observation
❑ Phone Call ❑ Conference
❑ E-mail ❑ Other _____

Questions/Issues to Address with Mentee:

Ideas Generated During Interaction:

Practical Applications:

*This form is to be duplicated as many times as needed. Create a section in your portfolio to file all interaction documentation.

Interactions Contact Log*

Date	Meeting Time	Total Time	Contact Initiated By Mentor Teacher or Mentee Teacher	Type of Contact One-on-One/Phone Call/ E-mail/Journal/Drop-in Visit/ Classroom Observation/ Conference/Other

*This form is to be duplicated as many times as needed. Create a section in your portfolio to file all interaction documentation.

COPYRIGHT © KENDALL/HUNT PUBLISHING COMPANY   Permission to duplicate for personal, non-commercial use.

Choice Activities for Ongoing Professional Development

CLASSROOM OBSERVATION

Invite mentee to observe in your classroom. Ask mentee to collect data in one area or skill of interest to you. Analyze the data together. Reminder: Modeling an open door to your classroom and to continuous improvement will promote the same from your mentee.

Build Reflective Practice
- Summarize insights gained from the observation.

INSTRUCTIONAL DESIGN ASSISTANCE

Co-plan a lesson or unit of instruction with mentee. Use opportunity to assess mentee's depth of instructional design and provide reinforcement and assistance as appropriate. After mentee teaches unit, debrief for continued professional growth.

Build Reflective Practice
- Document process.

RESOURCES FOR PROFESSIONAL DEVELOPMENT

Write up a list of professional resources and organizations that you use regularly for your own professional development.

Build Reflective Practice
- Share with your mentee and provide a copy for his/her use.

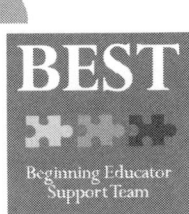

Second Thoughts: Journal Reflection

"He who dares to teach must never cease to learn." —ANONYMOUS

CHAPTER 6

Reflecting on the Mentoring Relationship

> "Some people come into our lives and quickly go . . .
> Some stay and leave footprints on our hearts
> and we are never, never the same."
>
> —Anonymous

As you anticipate the closure of another school year, you also anticipate what you have come to know as part of the cycle of teaching: end-of-year reports, closing out the year with students, creating meaningful learning opportunities to year-end, long-term planning for next year's curriculum, setting professional and personal goals for break. Your mentee may be a beginning teacher or a teacher new to your school community. Mentoring, through year-end, will involve providing logistics to provide a smooth closure. It also means providing a transition in your collegial relationship. Your mentee may be fluctuating between feelings of elation to end the year and feelings of loss with anticipation of departure of students. Realize as a mentor that this time can produce a change in emotion for your mentee. Continue to assess needs and adjust your mentoring for development. Your mentee may have become reliant on your professional relationship through the year. Reflect on the professional journey you have shared. Spend time discussing how your relationship will continue.

> "One reflects in order to see something that is not available to simple looking but requires the mirror of mind. What distinguishes reflection from memory is the hope that turning back upon oneself and the past will improve foresight."
>
> —Margret Buchmann

Devote conference time to review your mentee's progress this year. Use artifacts such as conference notes, feedback forms, interaction logs, evaluation instruments, classroom observation tools and choice activity documentation to celebrate growth. In addition, utilize reflection in all areas of teaching practice to identify a specific area for a professional growth goal for next school year. Remind mentee to check alignment with grade level/department, school and district pre-determined goals. Set your mentee up for continued success.

Duplicating the same synthesizing process, review your mentoring experience. Align new mentoring goals for the future to your knowledge and experience. Commit to being a teacher leader. As a mentor you educate, encourage and inspire. Celebrate!

- Celebrate your impact on teacher development; confidence and competence.
- Celebrate the influence you have had on student success.
- Celebrate the impression of mentoring on you professionally.
- Celebrate your commitment to the profession.

Tip from Mentor Teacher

"Now that you've experienced mentoring, recruit others to build school-wide collaboration and celebration of teaching practice."

- ❏ Plan continued partnership with mentee
- ❏ Advocate to administration ongoing mentee support
- ❏ Plan for summer professional growth
- ❏ Promote the benefits of the mentoring experience
- ❏ Report cards
- ❏ Cumulative folders
- ❏ Inventory
- ❏ Celebration ceremonies

Month _____

Sunday	Monday	Tuesday	Wednesday	Thursday	Friday	Saturday

Topics to Discuss with Mentee

- ❏ Share ideas and materials for ongoing learning to year end
- ❏ Reflection on year for professional growth plans for next year
- ❏ Classroom preparation for closing down the year

COPYRIGHT © KENDALL/HUNT PUBLISHING COMPANY

Professional Development Lesson Plan

TIP: Celebrate your mentee's year!
Plan for continued professional contact.

Subject: *Reflecting on the Mentoring Relationship*   Class/Period: *Seminar 6*   Date: _____

Objectives

- Analyze and reflect on mentoring practice.
- Design mentoring plan and tools for future implementation.
- Process ideas for and develop a professional growth plan for the upcoming school year.
- Celebrate success as a mentor.

Teaching Standard: *Engages in Professional Development*

Set *Read introduction to chapter.*

Procedures

1. Take time for a professional pause to reflect on the mentoring practices learned and generate an applied example from the following mentoring content:

    - Building the Relationship
    - Top Ten Needs
    - Phases of Teaching
    - Array Interaction Model
    - Reflective Questioning
    - The Mentoring Cycle
    - Characteristics of Mentoring
    - Teaching Standards
    - Facilitating Protégé Growth
    - Conferencing Strategies
    - Written and Verbal Feedback
    - Classroom Data Techniques

2. Complete *A Look Back: Mentor Reflection* (PR25) as you identify areas of professional growth specific to mentoring. This can be a nice inclusion in a portfolio or as an artifact to administration to showcase the importance of and your involvement in the mentoring process.

3. Generate strategies or create a document for future use in the four topic areas on *Close Down to Start Up* (PR 26). Two are designed to focus as you close down the year with your mentee. Two are designed for focus of an effective start in a new mentoring relationship. Remember: Once a mentor, always a mentor ☺. You are key to effective educational support and developing best practices in teaching. Allow your experiences of this year's mentoring to guide your ongoing development of your own mentoring and the professional development of more teachers.

Procedures (continued)

4. Plan a time to meet with your mentee with a specified agenda of planning meaningful learning for students to year-end. Also help design professional goals for summer and next year.

5. Turn back to PR17 in Chapter Three. Review your commitment to mentoring. Reflect on your progress toward goals set.

6. Take one step further in designing a mentoring plan by completing <u>The Future's Here: Professional Growth Plan</u> (PR27).

7. Design a special way to celebrate yourself and your mentee as you close out your year. More ideas in Choice Activities section.

Closure/Self-Assessment/Reflection	Celebration!
❏ Content Related Reflection ❏ Second Thoughts: Journal Reflection	❏

Extended Activities

❏ Mentor/Mentee Summary of Interaction
❏ Interactions Contact Log
❏ Choice Activities for Ongoing Professional Development

Note:
Practice ←
↓
Reflect
↓
Document
↓
Apply ─┘

Resources

❏ Calendar
❏ Tip
❏ Tip from Mentor Teacher
❏ Topics to Discuss with Mentee

Notes:

A Look Back: Mentor Reflection

Name _____ District _____

School _____ Grade Level/Content _____ Date _____

How have the experiences of mentoring increased your own teaching effectiveness?

List interpersonal/technical/content area skills you have developed or refined in the mentoring relationship(s)/training(s).

How have these skills impacted your competence in mentoring?

What are the benefits to you personally and/or professionally?

What was a mentoring situation that was challenging for you?

What mentoring skills did this situation require?

What was the outcome?

In what ways will you support and be an advocate for teachers in the future as a result of your mentor training/experience?

Close Down...

Strategies for Closure to the Mentoring Relationship	Ideas to Guide Mentee's Professional Development Plan

...to Start Up

Mentor/Mentee Partnership Agreement	Getting Acquainted Survey

PR26

The Future's Here: Professional Growth Plan

Brainstorm Box

What areas of professional growth should I consider as a mentor for next year?

Reminder: A Professional Growth Goal should link to student achievement.

Draft Box

Projected Professional Growth Goal

Methods Box

Potential Strategies for Attaining Professional Growth Goal

Notes:
- Check for alignment of your goal to possible district, school, department/grade level goals.
- Time activate this plan to be ready in final form for the beginning of the next school year.

Content Related Reflection

Refer back to Chapter One, *Content Related Reflection**. Read your responses reflecting your greatest strength and fear as you began mentoring. Respond with a reflection on your current perspective. Be specific with your areas of growth.

*Your *Content Related Reflection* from Chapter One and this reflection would be examples of growth to include in your professional portfolio.

Mentor/Mentee Summary of Interaction*

Mentor Teacher Information
Name _____
District _____
School _____
Grade Level/Content Area _____

Mentee Teacher Information
Name _____
District _____
School _____
Grade Level/Content Area _____

Contact Information
Date of Contact _____
   Beginning Time _____
   Ending Time _____
   Total Time _____

Contact Initiated By
❑ Mentor Teacher   ❑ Mentee Teacher

Type of Contact
❑ One-on-One   ❑ Drop-in Visit
❑ Journal   ❑ Classroom Observation
❑ Phone Call   ❑ Conference
❑ E-mail   ❑ Other _____

Questions/Issues to Address with Mentee:

Ideas Generated During Interaction:

Practical Applications:

*This form is to be duplicated as many times as needed. Create a section in your portfolio to file all interaction documentation.

COPYRIGHT © KENDALL/HUNT PUBLISHING COMPANY   Permission to duplicate for personal, non-commercial use.

Interactions Contact Log*

Date	Meeting Time	Total Time	Contact Initiated By Mentor Teacher or Mentee Teacher	Type of Contact One-on-One/Phone Call/ E-mail/Journal/Drop-in Visit/ Classroom Observation/ Conference/Other

*This form is to be duplicated as many times as needed. Create a section in your portfolio to file all interaction documentation.

Choice Activities for Ongoing Professional Development

CELEBRATION

Create a celebration activity for your mentee. For example, certificate, a special mentoring memory written in a card or framed, breakfast or lunch out, subscription to educational journal or provide a needed professional resource.

Build Reflective Practice
- Write a reflection of your year of mentoring and the impact on you and your mentee's professional growth. This is a celebration for you, too!

ASSISTANCE WITH DISTRICT PROCEDURES

Assist mentee with understanding or using district procedures for acquiring materials or services for next year. (Ideas include: warehouse order, professional growth courses, registration, budget request.)

Build Reflective Practice
- Reflect on the benefit to your school community of your practical assistance to your mentee.

*Suggestion: Create a quick reference procedure file for easy access when needed.

MY OWN CREATION

Design a professional growth choice activity for implementation at your site/district. Apply, reflect and share in the most beneficial way to mentees.

Second Thoughts: Journal Reflection

"I do the very best I know how; the very best I can; and I mean to keep on doing so until the end."
—ABRAHAM LINCOLN

Resources

Archer, J. (1999, March 17). New teachers abandon field at high rate. Education Week on the Web. Retrieved August 2, 1999, from the World Wide Web: http://www.edweek.org/ew/vol-18/27retain.h18

Association for Supervision and Curriculum Development. (1999). *Mentoring to improve schools.* Alexandria, VA.

Bey, T. & Holmes, T. (1990). *Mentoring: Developing successful new teachers.* Reston, VA: Association of Teacher Education.

Bluestein, J. (1989). *Being a successful teacher: A practical guide to instruction and management.* David S. Lake Publishers.

Brennan, S., Thames, W., & Roberts, R. (1999, May). Mentoring with a Mission. *Educational Leadership,* 49–52.

Carlie, B. (1999, June). *Facing a fierce forecast.* Arizona: Arizona School Administrators, Inc.

Checkley, K. & Rasmussen, K. (1999, January). Preparing two million: How districts and states attract and retain teachers. *Association for Supervision and Curriculum Development, 41* (1), 1–8.

Collins, C. (1987). *Time management for teachers: Practical techniques and skills that give you more time to teach.* Parker Publishing Company.

Creating a teacher mentoring program. NEA Foundation for Improvement of Education. Retrieved February 15, 2001, from the World Wide Web: http://www.nfie.org/publications/mentoring.htm

Danielson, C. (1996). *Enhancing professional practice: A framework for teaching.* Association for Supervision and Curriculum Development.

Darling-Hammond, L. (1997). *Doing what matters most: Investing in quality teaching.* New York: National Commission on Teaching and America's Future.

DeBruyn, R. (1997). *Welcome to teaching . . . and our schools.* Manhattan, KS: The MASTER Teacher, Inc.

Delgado, M. (1999). Lifesaving 101: How a veteran teacher can help a beginner. *Educational Leadership,* 27–29.

Enk, J. & Hendricks, M. (1981). *Shortcuts for teachers: Strategies for reducing classroom workload.* Pitman Learning, Inc.

Enz, B., Honaker, C., & Kortman, S. (2002). *Trade secrets for middle and secondary teachers.* Dubuque, IA: Kendall/Hunt Publishing Company.

Enz, B., Kortman, S., & Honaker, C. (2002). *Trade secrets for primary and elementary teachers.* Dubuque, IA: Kendall/Hunt Publishing Company.

Evans, T. (1996, September). Encouragement: the key to reforming classrooms. *Educational Leadership,* 81–85.

Fideler, E. & Haselkorn, D. (1998). *Learning the ropes: Urban teacher induction programs and practices in the United States.* Recruiting New Teachers, Inc.

Findley, D. & Findley, B. (1997). *Winding down the school year: A checklist for principals.* NASSP Bulletin: National Association of Secondary School Principals.

Fleming, D. (1996, September). Preamble to a more perfect classroom. *Educational Leadership International,* 73–76.

Fogarty, R. (1995). *Best practices for the learner centered classroom.* Arlington Heights, IL: IRI/SkyLight Training and Publishing, Inc.

Ganser, T. (1996). What do mentors say about mentoring? *Journal of Staff Development, 17* (3), 1–4.

Gless, J. & Moir, E. (2001, Winter). Teacher quality squared. *Journal of Staff Development, 22* (1), 62–65.

Gordon, S. (1991). *How to help beginning teachers succeed.* Alexandria, VA: Association for Supervision and Curriculum Development.

Hargreaves, A. & Fullan, M. (1999, June). Mentoring in the new millennium. *Theory Into Practice,* 3–8.

Harrison, A. & Burton, S. (1983). *Hot tips for teachers: A collection of classroom management ideas.* David S. Lake Publishers.

Hirsh, S. (1990, Fall). Designing induction programs with the beginning teacher in mind. *Journal of Staff Development, 11,* 24–26.

Huling-Austin, L., Odell, S., Ishler, P., Kay, R. & Edelfelt, R. (1989). *Assisting the beginning teacher.* Reston, VA: Association of Teacher Education.

Janas, M. (1996, Fall). Mentoring the mentor: a challenge for staff development. *Journal of Staff Development, 17* (4), 2–5.

Kohn, A. (1996, September). What to look for in a classroom. *Educational Leadership,* 54–55.

Kortman, S. & Honaker, C. (2002). *The BEST beginning teacher experience: A framework for professional development.* Dubuque, IA: Kendall/Hunt Publishing Company.

Kortman, S. & Honaker, C. (2002). *The BEST beginning teacher experience: Program facilitator guide.* Dubuque, IA: Kendall/Hunt Publishing Company.

Kortman, S. & Honaker, C. (2002). *The BEST mentoring experience: Program facilitator guide.* Dubuque, IA: Kendall/Hunt Publishing Company.

Lee, G. & Barnett, B. (1994, Winter). Using reflective questioning to promote collaborative dialogue. *Journal of Staff Development, 15* (1), 16–21.

Lewis, C., Schaps, E., & Watson, M. (1996, September). The caring classroom's academic edge. *Educational Leadership,* 16–21.

National Board for Professional Teaching Standards. (1999). *What teachers should know and be able to do.* Arlington, VA.

National Commission on Teaching and America's Future. (1996). *What matters most: Teaching for America's future.* New York.

National Evaluation Systems. (1997). *The induction years: The beginning teacher.* Amherst, MA.

NEA Today. (1998, November). *Helping new teachers succeed, 17* (3). (Videotape).

Noguera, P. (2000, May). Equity in education: what difference can teachers make? *California Professional Development Consortia,* 9–16.

Odell, S. & Huling, L. (2000). *Quality mentoring for novice teachers.* Indianapolis, IN: Kappa Delta Pi International Honor Society in Education.

Olsen, L. (2000, May). Accountability to whom for what? Steering a straight course. *California Curriculum News Report,* 6–7.

Porter, H. (1998). *Mentoring new teachers.* Thousand Oaks, CA: Corwin Press, Inc.

Reed, J. (2000). The importance of professional development for teachers. *Educational Horizons, 78* (3), 117–118.

Sack, J. (1999, March 24). All classes of special ed. teachers in demand throughout nation. Education Week on the Web. Retrieved August 2, 1999, from the World Wide Web: http://www.edweek.org/ew/vol-18/28speced.h18

Scherer, M. (1999). *A better beginning: Supporting and mentoring new teachers.* Alexandria, VA: Association for Supervision and Curriculum Development.

Stone, R. (1999). *Best classroom practices: What award winning elementary teachers do.* Thousand Oaks, CA: Corwin Press, Inc.

Strohmer, J. (1997). *Time-saving tips for teachers.* Thousand Oaks, CA: Corwin Press, Inc.

Thies-Sprinthall, L., & Gerler Jr., E. (1990, Fall). Support groups for novice teachers. *Journal of Staff Development, 11* (4), 18–22.

Tomlinson, C. (1995). *How to differentiate instruction in mixed ability classrooms.* Alexandria, VA: Association for Supervision and Curriculum Development.

Tomlinson, C. (1999, September). Mapping a route toward differentiated instruction. *Educational Leadership.* Alexandria, VA: Association for Supervision and Curriculum Development.

U.S. Department of Education, Office of Educational Research and Improvement. (1998). *Toward better teaching: Professional development in 1993–94,* NCES 98-230. Washington, DC.

Veenman, S. (1984). Perceived problems of beginning teachers. *Review of Educational Research, 54* (2), 143–178.

Whitaker, T., Whitaker, B. & Lumpa, D. (2000). *Motivating and inspiring teachers.* Larchmont, NY: Eye on Education, Inc.

Zachlod, M. (1996, September). Room to grow. *Educational Leadership,* 50–53.

Zemelman, S., Daniels, H. & Hyde, A. (1998). *Best practice: New standards for teaching and learning in America's schools (2nd ed.).* Portsmouth, NH: Heinemann.